Great
Grandfather
Spirit

Great Grandfather Spirit

A pathway to the source of
Native American wisdom

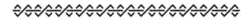

Wa-Na-Nee-Che
and Brid Fitzpatrick

Thorsons

Thorsons
An Imprint of HarperCollins*Publishers*
77—85 Fulham Palace Road
Hammersmith, London W6 8JB

The Thorsons website address is: www.thorsons.com

Published by Thorsons 2000

3 5 7 9 10 8 6 4

A catalogue record for this book
is available from the British Library

ISBN 0 7225 3964 9

Printed and bound in Great Britain by
Martins the Printers Ltd, Berwick upon Tweed.

Contents

Acknowledgements

We would like to thank the many people that support Wa-Na-Nee-Che's work, with special thanks to Grizzly, Hazel Perry, Barry Williams, Jim Brierley, Zena Corke, Sue Holdridge and Wendy Millar.

Further thanks to Nicola Graydon for her enthusiasm and support when first presented with the book and to our editor, Fiona Brown.

We acknowledge with gratitude permission received from Element Books Ltd to use material from *The Little Book of Native American Wisdom* by Steven McFadden.

About the Authors

Bríd Fitzpatrick was born on the West Coast of Ireland. Later she moved to London and toured as an actress. Bríd read English at Birkbeck College, University of London, followed by an MA in TV Drama at Goldsmiths' College. In 1998, Bríd wrote, produced and directed a film *Waves Without Sound*. This film is represented by the British Council and has been screened at international film festivals. She has since written another screenplay. Bríd has travelled extensively, including touring America where she visited numerous Native American reservations.

◄

Wa-Na-Nee-Che is of the Ojibway nation and he was raised on Turtle Mountain reservation in North Dakota. The energy and knowledge of the Old Ways were given to him primarily through visions. He has co-written *Principles of Native American Spirituality* and *White Eagle Medicine Wheel*, and he has recorded a healing meditation CD, *Journey Within*. Wa-Na-Nee-Che has also appeared on BBC Knowledge television, and various BBC radio programmes, discussing his spiritual pathway. Wa-Na-Nee-Che travels widely, sharing his spiritual message and helping people to reconnect with the Energy Source.

foreword

BRÍD FITZPATRICK

I have been fortunate enough to travel to the heart-lands of Turtle Island (America). I have been privileged to spend time amongst the Native American people upon grounds known as Indian reservations. As I grew more familiar with the diverse nations and made friends with members of the Ojibway, Lakota Sioux, Blackfoot, Apache and Cree, I became increasingly aware of their underlying need to re-connect with their ancestral spiritual pathway. They were looking back to find their way forward.

Wa-Na-Nee-Che is actively working towards this re-connection as he shares his words of wisdom, ancient knowledge and visions. He asked me if I would put pen to paper in an effort to help him bring his message of the Old Ways to the people. Wa-Na-Nee-Che spoke about the Energies, the spirits and Mother Earth. He said, 'All life, space and time revolves in and around the Energy Source emanating from the Creator.' As his words flowed, I began to write…

Introduction

A long, long time ago, many moons past, all people were one, all people were free and lived in harmony, understanding the power of the Creator, the Energy Source and the spirit. This time is way back, long before the Spanish Wars, long before the West was lost or world wars began. This time I speak of, my friends, is at the dawn of the two leggeds when you and I understood ourselves, each other and our great Mother, the Earth.

Over time, changes came and the people lost their way upon the spiritual pathway. The two leggeds divided the Family into groups, tribes, races and nations. Then the battle began within the hearts of many people against themselves. The energy connection was lost and the spirit was ignored. The spiritual life was abandoned. The mind and the physical skills of the body became dominant.

Many two leggeds in North and South America, the Native People, kept to the Old Ways and still understood the omnipotent power of the Creator and the Energy Source. They continued to listen and to talk to Mother Earth; although they too had divided, they had not forgotten the true Energies.

Many, many years have passed, many moons have come and gone, the two leggeds are not as one any more and there is no harmony. Mother Earth is dying. I hear her crying in the night like a wounded animal and I can smell the gases that have poisoned her body.

I shall take you back, with the help of Great Grandfather Spirit, to a time of peace and harmony that was central to the Old Ways. We will explain how many things began, based upon the protection of Mother Earth. We will journey to a time when Mother Earth was cared for with love and understanding; how she flourished in those days. This knowledge must be shared with everyone, so that we may all understand and the healing can begin.

You will also learn sacred prayers, rituals and ceremonies. The Great Grandfather Spirit and I will take you to the heart of the Sacred Sweat Lodge, the Sacred Channupa (Pipe) and the Vision Quest. All of this will help you on your journey. This information is not the domain of one race or culture, but of all two leggeds. We need to return as one people to the spiritual pathway that will ultimately help us to find the deepest part of ourselves.

It is time to share the wisdom that some people still practise upon Turtle Island (America). It is time to return to the Old Ways and I trust that only those with pure intentions and good hearts will be able to communicate the message to the Great Spirit, to the Creator and to the Energies. It is time to come together to honour and nurture our Mother, the Earth.

MY WORDS

I have no country,
I am of the earth.
Mother Earth is my home.
Wherever I stand,
Or lay my head to sleep,
I am at home.
I belong to the Human Race,
The two legged.
I am of but one colour, Red,
For this is the colour of our blood,
My brothers and sisters,
Grandfathers and Grandmothers.

I am of the spirit,
Of the mountains and the prairies,
The sea, the river and brook.
The rocks and trees are my closest friends.
My name is Wa-Na-Nee-Che,
This name has been given to me.
Its meaning shows me myself
'One Who is Needed by the People'.

There are many ways to pray, many words you can use and many things you can ask for, yet people often forget the first prayer, a prayer of thanks and offering. When I am asked how I pray, I answer, 'From my heart'. Before, during and after every single ceremony I perform, I offer sacred prayers from my heart.

OPENING PRAYER

Creator, I come before you in a humble way,
I thank you for this day.
I give thanks to the four directions and the four winds.
I give thanks for allowing me one more day to walk upon my Mother,
the Earth.

Creator, I give greetings to Mother Earth,
I ask her to continue to sustain me and all other life.
I tell her that one day my body will return to her.

Creator, I thank you and give greetings to Grandfather Sky.
I give thanks for the warmth father sun brings as
he travels from the east down to the west.
I give thanks for the light that allows me to see the great beauty
of Mother Earth.

Creator, I give thanks and ask you to watch over my relatives,
the four leggeds.
I give thanks for all they have taught me and my ancestors.
I give thanks for what they have given us.

Creator, I give thanks for the birds, the winged ones.
I give thanks for their beauty and songs that fill the air.
I honour the trees and the healing plants and herbs
that hold so much knowledge of life and are our guardians.
I give thanks for all they have taught us and still today,
they continue to teach.

Creator, for the water, the giver of life I give great thanks indeed.
I give thanks for all that is on, above, below and upon Mother Earth.

Creator, my most humble prayer is for the two leggeds, the human beings.
They are out of balance and need to return to the Old Ways,
To find love, harmony, peace and spiritual awakening.
I ask you, Creator, to reach down and touch our hearts
so that we can all live the good life
before the pathway of this life is no more.

Creator, Energies, accept my love, continue to walk with me upon this
pathway and help me in my work.
For it is the work of every living being, to help and love each other.
I give thanks.

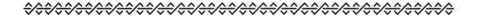

The First Breath of Turtle Island

GRANDFATHER
Look at our brokenness.
We know that in all Creation,
Only the human family
Has strayed from the Sacred Way.

We know that we are the ones
Who are divided
And we are the ones
Who must come back together
To walk in the Sacred Way.

Grandfather, Sacred One,
Teach us love, compassion, honour
That we may heal the earth
And heal each other.
OJIBWAY PRAYER

The Great Grandfather Spirit first came to me on the vision plane many years ago. Sometimes, it feels as though he has always been with me. I was on Turtle Mountain reservation at the time of this vision in my old home. The Great Grandfather Spirit appeared before me on the vision plane as an ancient man with long, flowing white hair that fell like silk around his wise, aged face. His face was mapped with his earth journey and lines ran across his cheeks and forehead like rivers through the land. I understood this was how the Great Grandfather had looked in his last days upon Mother Earth when he was a two legged. His deep, dark brown eyes oveflowed with knowledge from the energy of the Old Ways. Those gentle pools of wisdom have taught me many things over the years as the Great Grandfather Spirit's tall, thin frame beckons and guides me through vision after vision.

The first time the Great Grandfather Spirit's energy called me upon the vision plane, he spoke about the birth of a boy, his great grandson when they had all lived as a family upon Mother Earth. Over time, through visions without number, I have been shown the Old Ways through the eyes of a young boy and the wisdom of an Elder; the Great Grandfather Spirit.

I will share these visions and knowledge of the Great Grandfather Spirit with you. I will start with my first vision, the birth of the great grandson. Later, I will open my heart and invite you to understand many ancient and powerful ceremonies and rituals; all I ask is that you honour my trust.

The ceremonies, rituals, visions, animal connections and herbal remedies are intrinsic to the spirit of all Native American people, although I have specified some nations in reference to particular myths and spiritual practices. Furthermore, on a wider, more universal level, the spiritual and energy connections are integral to all human beings; to every two legged who breathes upon Mother Earth.

In times past, all the two leggeds of Mother Earth called upon a Higher Power and performed ceremonies and rituals to aid energy connection. The need for spiritual enlightenment continues to burn within the hearts of all two leggeds, and although I pertain to the Native American people, spiritually, I include all two leggeds, for we are all related and dependent upon each other to unite our energy force and honour all living things.

❖❖❖❖❖❖❖❖❖❖❖❖❖❖❖❖❖❖❖❖❖❖❖❖❖❖❖❖❖❖❖❖❖❖

The first lesson is that all ceremonies and rituals must be performed with a pure and compassionate heart. It is only with honourable intentions and compassion that you can truly journey upon the vision plane and connect with the Energy Source.

◂

As I lay sleeping on that freezing cold winter's night on Turtle Mountain reservation, I was grateful for the warmth of my bedroom. My spirit was freed the moment consciousness fell away and I was taken into the vision world.

I was walking, walking slowly upon a long, windy road. I could hear the wind whistling through the trees, but I could not see any trees. It was barren and arid all around me, but I was not afraid. I felt as though the dust beneath my feet was speaking to me, urging me on and helping me upon my pathway.

Sunshine pushed through and diffused the blue-white clouds. I felt a presence, an energy walking beside me. When I looked to my left, I saw the willowy figure of an ancient man. I slowed my pace and he slowed with me, then he beckoned with his hand and two rocks appeared. We sat upon the rocks. The Great Grandfather Spirit smiled at me and raised his hand in the air, 'I need to speak to you my friend. There is much I wish to teach you as only the Energies can. Are you willing to understand?' I nodded, then the Elder put his hands upon my shoulders, and as he looked into my eyes I began to feel energized. Then he began to explain Energy.

The Great Grandfather spoke of a time upon Mother Earth, long since past, when a young woman was about to become a mother. The Great Grandfather Spirit said that the honey-skinned youth was scarcely sixteen summers, but she was ready for the child she knew had chosen her to be his mother. She had seen her firstborn in a vision two summers before. Beads of sweat softened her brow as she placed her hands upon her swollen stomach and waited.

The Great Grandfather Spirit circled his hand in the air as he described a swirling energy force that curled and rose high above the birthing mother's

❖❖❖❖❖❖❖❖❖❖❖❖❖❖❖❖❖❖❖❖❖❖❖❖❖❖❖❖❖❖❖❖❖❖

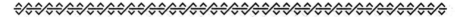

head. A streak of violet blue shot out of the dancing Energy and blazed brilliant light across the grey night sky. The Great Grandfather Spirit said it was the child's energy, as new life prepared for his journey to Mother Earth.

The child's energy had also come to the Great Grandfather Spirit in a vision long before his birth and spoke of the remarkable friendship that would grow between them. In the vision, the colour and sound of energy shone and bounced in many different directions: the Great Grandfather Spirit followed the energy, and at the same time, he felt as though he led the powerful force.

The exchange of energy brought great knowledge, but the Great Grandfather Spirit already understood that we are all one. We are energy. The Energy Source sent us here and our own energy chose to walk upon Mother Earth.

The Great Grandfather Spirit said, 'The boy-child's journey to the Mother Earth was almost completed. Thunder roared and as a streak of blue lightning hit the earth, the child was born, but his energy had arrived before him.' The Great Grandfather smiled and tears of happiness welled in his eyes as the poignant memory touched his spirit and he lived within that moment again.

The Great Grandfather Spirit opened his hand and revealed a pinch of tobacco, 'This is what I offered in thanks for the safe arrival of my great grandchild. I offered the tobacco to honour the Creator and the Energies that had brought this baby safely to the heart of our family. This was a common practice of gratitude in the Old Ways.

'In the days and years that were to follow I would teach the young boy a great many things, but he would also be my teacher,' the Great Grandfather Spirit nodded. 'Our energies were perfectly balanced. The relationship created a space and time, which was also created for us and within this sacred place of being, Turtle Island, we grew together.

'My great grandson's curiosity increased with each passing year. By his fifth summer, he was ready to hear the story of creation. I remember his questions, "Why do we live on Turtle Island? Who made it a turtle? How were we created?" ' The Great Grandfather laughed gently as he spoke of this.

Then he looked into my eyes and my energy slipped away and I was back upon Turtle Mountain reservation with the image of the Great Grandfather Spirit and his words still whispering in the wind. As I sat up and drew a blanket around me, the turtle energy felt close and the creation stories I had heard since I was a boy gathered around me in the early morning light.

There are many variations of creation stories told and re-told by the Native American people. Often, these stories feel as ancient as the earth herself. Great Great Grandparents, Great Grandparents and Grandparents have taught their grandchildren about the Creator, the Energy Source and Mother Earth through these stories as they sat around warm campfires on cold, winter nights. Every nation has its own story, but there are similarities between each one.

The most significant similarity between these stories is that the animals, our four-legged friends, the flying, swimming and crawling ones, were all on Mother Earth before us. Therefore, they deserve to be placed at the top of the totem pole and we, the human beings at the bottom. The animals are our teachers. They are in tune with themselves, their energy and Mother Earth. Animals can sense the presence of a spirit or other energy forms, because they understand the connection to the Energy Source. The animal energy is alert and works on many different levels, whilst we humans have blocked much of our way to the true Energy core. Therefore, most of us cannot find our own pathway on this earth walk. The creation stories stem from the Spirit World and teach us about the omnipotence of the Creator and the power of the Energy Source.

THE OJIBWAY CREATION MYTH

The Ojibway's creation myth begins with a blazing fire that rushed out of the stars, ignited by great gusts of energy. It is said that the fire created masses of bright orange, molten lava, which ran wild like a raging fever. The Creator then poured pure water upon the fire to cool its scorching heat. Mountains, valleys and plains grew from the water's calming touch. There was fire, water and earth, but no air to breathe. The Creator blew gently upon the earth and the air opened the earth's lungs as she took her first breath of life.

Seeds were dropped upon the earth and the air became wind and scattered the seeds to the four directions. Trees shot up into the sky and were given sacred powers as they would become the caretakers of the air and grandparents to all beings. Trees would also be known as the standing people.

The standing people were given the first knowledge, the energy of all life, and they were asked to pass their energy on to all other living things. Plants and herbs grew from the shade and air provided by the trees. The plants and herbs held the energy of healing and life-giving forces, which in time would help to save many lives.

The Ojibway believe that tobacco was the first plant to grow and that this plant possesses many strong healing properties. The tobacco plant is still honoured today as the first plant and continues to be used as a spiritual offering to the Creator and the Energies.

Later, the rocks and stones, the sitting people, would give rich minerals to the human beings, the two leggeds. The sitting ones would also provide shelter for all; the two leggeds, the four leggeds, the flying, swimming and crawling ones.

The Energies were ready to form the totem pole. At that time, in the beginning of light, life flowed easily and everything was in perfect harmony upon Mother Earth. The earth was ready for new life. It was time to create animals, the four leggeds and other life forms: the flying, swimming and crawling ones. They would populate Mother Earth and be placed near the top of the totem pole after plant life. The turtle was the first to be created and from her energy, many others were given life. The myth claims that Turtle Island (America) was built upon the back of a turtle. The turtle energy continues to touch the hearts of the indigenous people today as we still call America by her first name, Turtle Island. In this way, the turtle is always honoured as a significant and ancient, sacred swimming one.

In keeping with the Ojibway myth, many four leggeds, flying, swimming and crawling ones came after the turtle. New life blended their energy as one and settled into the warm embrace of Mother Earth. The Creator wanted to add one more energy form to his new creation and so human beings, the two leggeds, were born. Thus, they were placed at the bottom of the totem pole as the last life energy to be created. The animals helped to create the two leggeds, as they were on earth before us.

The myth claims that the four leggeds and all other life forms extended their energy and became one with the new energy, the human beings. They understood the needs and limitations of the two leggeds and that is why nature and animals never judge or criticize the two leggeds.

At first, the two leggeds were respectful and grateful to be upon Mother Earth. The new human beings were seen as caretakers and they felt honoured by their position. The two leggeds cared for the earth as their mother. They also cared for each other and their four-legged family. They understood the energy connection and that all living things were one, created from the Energy Source.

Sadly, the Ojibway myth changes from happiness to sorrow as moons glided over moons and things began to change, people divided into tribes, nations, cultures and races. The division caused friction and distrust in the family. Arguments sprung from fear, but they soon turned to greed and aggression that led to wars.

Mother Earth began to suffer as the two leggeds' hostility and greed increased. The energy twisted and turned, trying to ease itself back into a natural, gentle flow as before, but it was trapped as many had blocked their own connection to the Energy Source.

The two leggeds did not call upon the Creator or the Energies any more, and so the situation worsened. In the years ahead, the two leggeds would forget about the Energy connection altogether. The Energy connection would lose all meaning and it would take many, many moons before the power of Energy would even be recognized again.

By that time, Mother Earth would be scarred and butchered from their battles and plundered for her riches. It would take as much time to heal her as it did to hurt her. The myth warns that time may not be on the side of the human beings, the foolish two leggeds. Yet the myth promises hope if a great surge of energy from all humankind re-connects with the Source and returns to the harmonious Old Ways where healing can begin. The Ojibway Creation Myth asks us to call upon the turtle energy to help us find our way back upon the true pathway.

Turtle Birth Ceremony

The Ojibway, Ottawa and Potawtomi nations revere the turtle as the heart of the earth we walk upon. The sacred swimming one is associated with birth and life itself. The turtle is seen as part of the womb of Mother Earth and it is celebrated in many special turtle sweat lodge ceremonies. The turtle is also utilized in birth ceremonies to celebrate, honour and protect the new-born baby.

If the parents of a new-born baby wish to have the Turtle Birth Ceremony performed for their child, then they must seek a medicine person or spiritual adviser to help them initiate this ancient ritual. A tiny piece of the baby's umbilical cord is utilized by the medicine person or spiritual adviser when it detaches naturally from the baby. It is believed the baby's purest energy is caught within the cord.

During the time of the Old Ways, the turtle offered its life and a shell was made available to the medicine person. Today, a picture of a turtle or some other turtle artefact is often used to represent the turtle's energy. The cord is united with the turtle's energy as the turtle artefact and the cord are bound together inside a leather medicine bag. The Turtle Birth Ceremony usually takes place in a natural environment by the sea, a lake or a river, honouring the turtle and the child's connection to water. The medicine person or spiritual adviser calls upon the Creator, the Energies and the ancestors of the turtles as he or she prays for the child's protection and guidance upon the earth pathway. Sacred tobacco is offered to the four directions and sage is burned to cleanse any negative energies.

The parents safeguard the medicine bag filled with sacred turtle energy until the time comes for the child to accept its contents. It is believed that the Turtle Birth Ceremony gives the child a strong connection to mother turtle and their energies remain united throughout the two legged's life.

If you are unable to locate a medicine person or spiritual adviser and you wish to carry out a Turtle Birth Ceremony, it is possible for you to perform a similar ceremony independently. It must be stressed that a pure and compassionate heart is essential when performing rituals and ceremonies. Sacred plants, herbs and artefacts are powerful tools that can aid ceremonies and help to connect us with the Energy Source. The following offers advice on the performing the Turtle Birth Ceremony without assistance from a medicine person or a spiritual adviser. The tobacco offerings and sacred sage smudging are integral components of all rituals and ceremonies that I perform.

I believe it is necessary to honour the Creator, Energies and four directions before proceeding with any ritual or ceremony. It is equally important to smudge the area and whoever is present to rid the atmosphere and two leggeds of negative energies and surround them with a protective shield of sage smoke.

CEREMONIAL AND RITUAL PREPARATION

It is advisable to hold sacred rituals and ceremonies in a location, internally or externally, that speaks to your heart and feels right for you. It is important to feel comfortable and safe wherever you choose to perform a ritual or a ceremony. Once the location is decided upon, an offering of tobacco must be made to honour the Creator and the Energies. A pinch of tobacco is sufficient for each offering. The first pinch of tobacco is offered by raising your arm towards grandfather sky. Prayers of gratitude are given to the Creator for the miracle of life, energy and Mother Earth. The next pinch of tobacco is offered to Mother Earth and laid upon her as you touch the ground or floor.

Then a pinch of tobacco is given to each of the four directions. It is up to each individual to decide upon the direction of the first offering. I often begin with the north and a pinch of tobacco is placed upon the floor or ground facing north. Pray to the north and honour it with thanks. Likewise, honour the east, south and west in a sun-wise (clockwise) direction with prayers of gratitude. The four directions are honoured and given thanks for the earth balance and energy provided by each direction.

After the tobacco offerings have been completed, it is time to call upon the sacred sage plant to smudge the appointed place of ceremony. Each person, artefact and all objects must be smudged as well. The sage utilized in smudging and healing must be picked with ceremony and prayers.

It is imperative that sage is honoured with ancient rituals and prayers before it is taken from its natural home. Consent must be obtained from the sage leaves by speaking with the sacred plant's energy and gaining permission to use it (see Chapter 8).

Take a small handful of the sacred sage in your left hand and roll it into a ball with your right hand. The left hand is closest to your heart and will connect your heart-energy directly with the sage. Then place the sage ball in a scallop shell or a fire resistant container. This is known as a smudge bowl. Light the sacred sage and gently blow into the sage ball until the cleansing smoke rises. (To smudge a person or an object, the smoke should be wafted in their direction with, ideally, a feather.) Then walk in a sun-wise position, honouring each of the four directions. Again, the first direction you choose to begin depends upon where your energy is pulled. As you walk with the burning sage in the smudge bowl, pray and call upon the Creator and Energies to cleanse the space, each person, and the artefacts and objects you intend to use upon your altar at a later stage. Ask the sage to bring good energies, protection and connection to you and all in the chosen space.

When you have completed your circular walk, then smudge all those present, including artefacts and objects. Last of all, smudge yourself, allowing the sacred sage smoke to drift from your feet to your head as you pray and ask for the good Energies to guide you throughout the ceremony. Lay the sage bowl near the altar and allow the rest of the sage to burn off naturally as you proceed with the ceremony.

After smudging, a ceremonial altar is prepared. The altar is usually placed upon a blue or white cloth. The colour of the cloth is significant, as each colour has different energy vibrations. A blue cloth represents energy spirit and healing. A white cloth symbolizes the purity and balance of new life. Then objects and artefacts that are precious and meaningful are chosen and placed upon the cloth. You may also want to place a bowl of water upon the altar to honour the turtle and the new-born baby's connection to water. Other sacred objects and tools can be added such as feathers, crystals and stones.

As you lay each artefact upon the altar, pray and call upon the energy of the turtle and all the turtle ancestors. Place the turtle artefact in the centre of the altar. Ask for spiritual assistance to guide you through the Turtle Birth Ceremony. When you are satisfied that the altar is ready, give thanks and offer a pinch of tobacco to the four directions in a sun-wise position upon the altar itself. Reserve a pinch of tobacco to be placed upon the turtle artefact in the middle of the altar.

Chanting or singing can raise the energy and help to connect with the Energy Source. As you chant or sing, make the sounds joyful as you call in the turtle and ancestral energy. Then place a small piece of the baby's umbilical cord upon the central turtle artefact and pray for the child protection and guidance upon its earth walk. Ask the turtle energy to use its shell to protect the child whenever extra shelter is needed in the course of his or her earth life. Ask the turtle energy to share its balance and oneness with nature with the two legged whose energy it now shares from the heart.

Give thanks to the turtle energy for allowing you to call upon it. The circular completion of the Turtle Birth Ceremony involves more prayers of gratitude as thanks are offered to the Creator, the Energies and the turtle.

The altar can remain undisturbed for four days and four nights. This allows the Energies to continue to work with the ceremonial prayers and requests. Visions can also be induced by leaving the altar to work with the turtle energy upon the altar for a further four days and nights.

Or you may choose to remove it immediately after the Turtle Birth Ceremony is finished. Whether you remove the altar immediately after the ceremony or choose to leave it for four days and nights, the same procedure applies when the altar is taken down. Take the central turtle artefact from the altar, retaining the tobacco attached to it. Place the turtle artefact and tobacco into a small, leather medicine bag and secure it with prayers for the new-born child. When the child is older, he or she may wish to wear the medicine bag or keep it close to them.

All other artefacts and objects should be removed one by one, praying and honouring them for enabling the Turtle Birth Ceremony. Put each artefact in a safe place to be utilized again if required. The cloth needs to be carefully folded and placed close to the artefacts used in the ceremony.

A child who has had the Turtle Birth Ceremony performed can easily call upon the turtle's energy when help or guidance is needed as he or she matures. The child may also feel the energy of water as an integral part of its being.

We are all connected to animal energies and their power. As illustrated, ceremonies and rituals can be utilized to guide and help us. Throughout this book, ancient ceremonies and rituals are shared to re-direct us back to the Energy Source, often with the aid of totem animals. In order to access the deepest spiritual place within ourselves, it is often necessary to call upon the animals, the four leggeds, flying, swimming and crawling ones. The animals have not lost their energy connection, it is only the two leggeds who have difficulty re-connecting with the Energy Source.

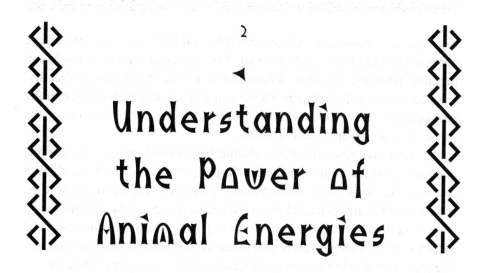

2

Understanding the Power of Animal Energies

If you talk to the animals
They will talk with you,
And you will know each other.
If you do not talk to them
You will not know them,
And what you do not know you will fear.
What one fears, one destroys.
CHIEF DAN GEORGE — COAST SALISH

In my second vision, the Great Grandfather Spirit's energy beckoned me towards a watery light. I could see different animals, four leggeds, flying, swimming and crawling ones. Later, I would come to understand the power of animal energies. I was upon a new pathway this time, trees and plant life surrounded me as my energy floated towards the light. I was led by an unseen Energy towards a pond of water. As I walked towards the pond, I looked towards grandfather sky; half the sky was made up of bright yellow-flooded sunshine and the other half was dark with mud-coloured clouds. It felt ominous to me, but the Great Grandfather Spirit signalled to me and the sky's shadowed world receded. This time I could see Great Grandfather Spirit in the distance beside the pond and he waved as I approached him.

We greeted each other like old friends. The Great Grandfather Spirit said, 'The two leggeds ignore all the warnings their four-legged, flying, swimming and crawling friends try to give them. The humans believe themselves to be superior in their knowledge, yet it is the animals who can teach the two leggeds about Energy, the most vital source of all life.'

I listened carefully; I knew that each word held wisdom that I would need to help me upon my earthly pathway. The Great Grandfather Spirit pointed towards two rocks beside the pond and we sat down once again. The Great Grandfather Spirit spoke, 'The animals, trees, herbs, rocks and all forms of nature have been created to help the two leggeds survive and to find their true pathway upon Mother Earth.

'They are our teachers. In return for their wisdom and knowledge, the two leggeds are the caretakers of Mother Earth's children. It is not important whether they live beneath the earth, above the earth or upon the earth. Many two leggeds have forgotten the Old Ways. They have forgotten their duties as caretakers, yet the animals still try, hoping that the Energies will be understood and their message will be heard.'

The Great Grandfather Spirit had shared his knowledge, then he fell silent, shaking his head sadly. I thought I could see tears in the corners of his eyes when he finished speaking.

We sat silent for a long time, then he looked up and said, 'When my great grandson was born, he could not sit up, crawl or walk. Later, he ran everywhere. It is like that with the animals. When they come to you in visions or in real life, they try to teach you about your energy connection step by step. It takes time to learn and the two legged must learn the values of humility and patience.'

The Great Grandfather Spirit paused for a long time and I looked into the clear beauty of the pond. I could see the extraordinary split-sky mirrored in the water. I was about to ask the Great Grandfather what the sky colours meant, when he spoke again, 'Once, when my great grandson was about three summers, I could see that he understood the language of animals. I learnt many things by watching my great grandson talk to his four-legged friends. At that time, there was a half-dog, half-wolf wandering alone in the area. Sometimes, we would feed it. When this four legged was around, my great grandson would feel its energy before it came into sight, and he would go out to greet the four legged.

'I would follow him discreetly. The half-dog, half-wolf would come right up and stand in front of him and they would stare into each other's eyes, exchanging energy. As he grew older, the four legged disappeared and I never saw it again. Perhaps it still came to my great grandson in visions. Children often understand the power of animal energies and speak naturally to their four-legged friends. It is only when society closes in around them that their energy is blocked and the connection is broken.' The Great Grandfather nodded to me and laid his hand upon my head and a powerful energy surged.

Then I heard a heart-drum beat beneath our feet. The Great Grandfather Spirit closed his eyes. A soft chant echoed around us and the trees bowed their leafy heads as the old man sang and danced. The earth trembled a little and then a white horse appeared. The horse pranced back and forth as the chant grew louder. The milk-white horse reared onto its back legs and when it came back down to the grassy earth, it was a man. The chanting faded into the whiteness and the air was still. I looked at the man, white from his hair to his ice-pale feet. The snowy man raised his hands to his face and turned away. As he turned, he shape-shifted back into the form of a white horse and galloped with the energy of the air.

I looked at the Great Grandfather Spirit and he disappeared like a ripple in a pond. The half-painted sky darkened and the sun disappeared. I sat in the darkness. I could feel a cold energy brushing against my face. I woke up and the wind had blown my window wide open and there was a scattering of leaves on the floor. As I looked closer, I realized they had settled in the form of a buffalo.

In present times, you can still hear about shape shifters and skin walkers. Shape shifters are revered because of their energy connection and they are also known to use their energy wisely. Conversely, skin walkers have a negative energy attached to them. Native American nations from the South West of Turtle Island are extremely fearful of skin walkers. It is said that the skin walkers steal power by digging up the graves of medicine people and removing their buried medicine bags. The medicine bags continue to hold the potency that the medicine people worked with when they walked upon Mother Earth.

It is believed that skin walkers can also take the shape of animals or other two leggeds for negative purposes. Energy is pure, but like all things, it can be utilized for good or bad. Many people in the modern world use energy in a negative way. There are a limitless number of ways to abuse energy: nuclear weapons, global pollution, rain forest destruction and animal vivisection, to name but a few. This is against the harmonious and natural flow of energy and nature. Animals do not share our mind control society and they utilize their energy instinctively.

After the second vision, many four leggeds, flying, swimming and crawling ones came to me and taught me how to connect with their energy. The Great Grandfather Spirit opened the doorway for their energies to come through and now they are essential teachers in my life. I was guided by the animal energies to share their wisdom in the *White Eagle Medicine Wheel* book. The illustrated animal cards within the *White Eagle Medicine Wheel* can help people connect with their totem animal, who ultimately leads them to their own source of power.

Historically, all Native American nations have relied upon the power of animal energies to guide them spiritually and also to help them find healing herbs and plants. They ask Gitchgee Manito (Ojibway for the Great Spirit) for a vision that will lead them to the power of the animal energy.

If you do not remember your own dreams and visions, there are other ways to become part of the animal and achieve its perfect sense of being and harmonious energy. Some people are drawn towards spirit paintings or sand paintings and these images can open a doorway to the animal Energies. You can also observe the animals, flying, swimming and crawling ones, imagine that you are part of their world and one of them. The alertness and speed of most four leggeds is far greater than that of a human being.

Their senses and energy are in tune and, by imagining you are whatever animal you have chosen, your energy is automatically joining their energy. Animals often try to contact us through energy, or some might say by using telepathy. It is from the same energy source and they often communicate with each other in this way. Have you ever sat upon a hill or walked softly upon a flowered floor in the forest? Have you ever been within your home and suddenly, you turn you head, convinced you have heard your name? The human response is usually to dismiss this subtle message and say, 'My mind is playing tricks.' What if it was not your mind, but the animal energies trying to contact you? Do you look to see where the voice is coming from, or do you just let it pass? If we listen more closely, maybe we can connect with the energy. Some people call this instinct or intuition, but I understand it as energy. Pay attention to the little voices, the sounds inside and outside, and you may find the answers you seek. Each animal — the four leggeds, flying, swimming and crawling ones — carries a different message and its own power. It comes to help you and to share its gift.

In visions, animals, the four leggeds, flying, swimming and crawling ones have symbolic meanings which may need to be interpreted. Many animals come in visions as energy guides, but they also come to warn us. Others bring different realizations and energy gifts. The most commonly vision cited four legged, flying, swimming and crawling ones, together with their symbolism and totem significance, are listed below. Although I have named specific Native American nations in relation to particular animal

connection and myths, I reiterate that all Native Americans have an ancient and intrinsic spiritual relationship with the four legged, flying, swimming and crawling ones.

THE WOLF

The Pawnee nation's myth of the Wolf Star is believed to be the origin of the Skidi Pawnee or Wolf Clan. The Pawnee myth tells of the magical energy of the thunderstorm, also known as Paruksti. It is said that Paruksti came out of the west to look upon creation. The grandparents and great grandparents of the Pawnee from further back than can be recalled talk of a time before creation, when the Energies forgot to invite the Wolf Star, Sirius, to help in the world's creation. The Wolf Star blamed Paruksti for this omission. The Wolf Star sent one of his energies, a wolf, to Mother Earth to follow Paruksti.

Paruksti carried the two leggeds in a whirlwind bag and when he wanted their company he would open the bag and the two leggeds would set up camp and hunt the buffalo. The Pawnee myth tells of how one day as Paruksti lay sleeping the wolf sent by the Wolf Star crept up and stole the whirlwind bag.

The wolf allowed the two leggeds out of the bag, but this time, they found themselves upon arid, barren ground. At first, they entertained the wolf, but upon discovery of his true identity, they killed him.

Paruksti was deeply saddened when he learned what had happened. He looked at the two leggeds, 'You have brought the cold hand of violence and destruction upon yourselves. Hereafter, you will be known as the Wolf Clan and you must honour his spirit by carrying a sacred bundle made of the wolf skin you have killed.'

The Pawnee myth embodies the spirit and energy of the wolf. In the Spirit World, problems are not resolved with violence. Today, the Pawnee and many other Native American nations still revere the wolf's energy.

The wolf is misunderstood and, as a result of human fear, it has been

annihilated in many parts of the world, including Turtle Island. Yet the wolf's energy remains intact; it is only the two legged who has lost the way.

If you have the opportunity to see wolves in the wild, then it is possible to observe their behaviour and learn from them. The same cannot be said about zoos or other places of enforced closure. Cages and bars maim the animals' spirits and disturbs the natural flow of energy.

It is difficult to find a safe, free place for wolves these days, maybe that is why they come in visions so often, connecting purely on an energy level. If a wolf comes to you in a vision, his or her message depends upon how he or she approaches you. The colour of the wolf is important as well. A dark grey wolf can represent danger or an enemy amongst people you already know and trust. It can also mean that there is a dark side within yourself that you need to understand more. A white wolf usually symbolizes a new dawn of enlightenment on a high spiritual level. If a wolf comes up behind you, you may need to guard your back, or learn to look behind you as well as in front.

If a wolf approaches you directly, then he or she is ready to make an energy connection. If a wolf looks into your eyes, it is giving you a part of its energy, and you must use it wisely. A pack of wolves represents your family, which may mean you are looking for a family of your own, or you may want to work on family relationships that you already have. Wolves are extremely intelligent and resourceful and these are gifts we can all share.

THE BEAR

The Blackfoot nation called upon a medicine man to contact the bear energy as they formed the Bear Clan. The Blackfoot medicine man imitated the energy of the bear through physical representation by wearing a bear skin. The Blackfoot nation believed the bear skin held the original bear's energy and it would naturally permeate the medicine man and blend with his energy. The medicine man's Bear Clan Ceremony would also illicit visions and provide spiritual enlightenment.

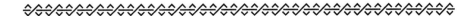

Within this spiritual connection to the bear, killing the bear was often prohibited. Instead, the Blackfoot nation waited for a bear to die naturally before removing its skin. They also used bear totems and artefacts to represent the bear energy.

Energy connection to the bear was highly prized as it promised bear strength and courage. The Blackfoot nation wore medicine bundles with bear artefacts inside to ward off negative energies. The medicine bundles also kept the bear energy physically and spiritually close to their hearts. The Blackfoot medicine bundle carrier honoured the bear as a fierce warrior. Bears still command respect and awe amongst the Blackfoot nations.

The wilderness that epitomized the bear's rambling nature is harder to find in present times. There is still some natural habitat for the bear upon Turtle Island, but more often they are designated to parks and other areas of enclosure. The bear's spirit is not easily resigned to smaller tracts of land and less natural food resources. The balance of the bear and nature has been fractured by human interference. The rapid population growth and creeping, land-ravenous cities have all but banished wild bears.

The two leggeds are often fearful of the bears' ferocious retaliation as a desperate, starving bear will occasionally attack a human being. But it is human imbalance that brought this indignity upon the bears as they fight for their own survival.

Yet, the bears are still willing to help the two leggeds as our visions contest. If a large grizzly bear is seen in a vision, it symbolizes the need for greater personal strength. It also reiterates your own power to walk upon the vision plane and gain spiritual enlightenment. The bear urges the person in the vision to embrace their own substantial power. If a brown bear appears, it also represents the need to be stronger spiritually, physically and mentally. The brown bear also signifies the need to protect oneself more through inner energy connection. The bear, like all four leggeds, is a teacher and a guide for the two leggeds.

THE EAGLE

The Hopi and Navaho nations celebrated the eagle energy in ceremonial eagle dances. They relied upon the strength and size of the eagle's magnificent wing span to be able to reach the Creator with their prayers. The Hopi and Navaho nations adorned themselves with eagle feathers as they spread out their arms and danced to transform themselves spiritually into the eagle's physical being and energy. The eagle dance would become increasingly energetic, until many felt their energy fly with the precision and grace of an eagle.

The eagle was perceived by the Hopi and Navaho nations as the most sacred of all flying beings. The eagle was recognized as a divine being with great powers that could be transferred onto the Hopi and Navaho nations through the eagle dance. They looked to the eagle to teach them about life and ultimately about themselves.

The Hopi and Navaho honoured the eagle as a skilful hunter with unusual gifts of observation and perception, as well as admirable physical strength.

Eagle totems such as eagle feathers, claws and artefacts were considered extremely valuable. Eagle feathers were awarded with ceremonial honour to those that displayed bravery or proved themselves valorous or especially spiritually connected. The Hopi and Navaho nations carry eagle totems to this day, and remain in awe of the power of the eagle energy.

Like his four-legged friends, the winged eagle has been endangered by the two leggeds who failed to understand the necessity of the eagle energy for all living things. Happily, work is now being carried out to protect the eagle so that we can continue to enjoy sightings of the sacred flying one, gliding across the blue skies as the eagle energy touches and brightens us.

If an eagle comes to you in a vision, it symbolizes great power and signals a radical change in your life. The eagle energy can help to carry your hopes to reality. The eagle energy represents freedom and suggests you spread your own wings spiritually. The golden eagle promises prosperity on all levels. If the eagle does not face you, it is seen as a warning and

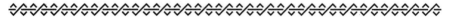

emphasizes the need to be more alert and observant before necessary changes can be realized.

The eagle energy is extremely powerful and will only join the vision world when it is vital to help the two leggeds.

THE DOG

The more domesticated animals, like the dog, were once regarded as sacred, particularly by the Sioux nations. The Sioux held many secret ceremonies in honour of the dog energy. They performed sacred dances to celebrate the dog and his unstinting loyalty. The details of these ceremonies are kept secret to the present day and that is to be respected. It is sufficient to say that the dog was one of the most honoured four legged of the Sioux nations.

It is also worth remembering that the Sioux nations relied upon the dog to work and enable them before the sacred dog (the horse) was made available to them. Today, it is less likely for the Sioux nations to honour the dog energy, although a number of Sioux medicine people still utilize the dog energy when performing sacred ceremonies.

When dogs visit us in visions, especially if the dog is black, it can be interpreted as the need to be wary of certain friends. Dogs often come in visions to protect our energy and we must pay attention to their warnings. Dogs can also represent a loved one in your life and herald the return of a lost love, especially if the dog holds something in its mouth. It is usually good news when a dog meets you in the vision world, particularly if the dog is light in colour. The dog energy embodies loyalty and faithfulness. You may need to be more loyal to your friends or seek out more loyal friends. If a dog lies by your side, then it symbolizes the blessing of true friendship.

THE BUTTERFLY AND DRAGONFLY

The Ojibway nation honours the butterfly and the dragonfly energy. This is reflected in some of their clothing designs, colours and artwork. The Ojibway nation believe that these beautiful, brightly coloured flying beings are important energy guides to be observed as teachers for the two leggeds. If you take the time to watch a butterfly or dragonfly, you will be hypnotized by its beauty and enthralled by its harmonious relationship with nature.

If the butterfly or dragonfly visits you in a vision, it can signify the beginning of new life. The flying colours can light the two leggeds' pathway and guide them upon their earth journey.

If the butterfly is seen in its warm cocoon, this means that the Energies are working with your own energy to prepare you for your pathway. When the butterfly is dusted with golden hues and the flying one's life spreads into a blaze of rainbow lights, this signifies that you are ready to be true to yourself and accept joy in your life. Butterfly and dragonfly energy is one of harmony and we can emulate their contented state of being. In waking time, if butterflies or dragonflies are in your area it is a sign of purity, as it means that the area is relatively free of pollution.

THE HUMMINGBIRD

The Ojibway nation sees the hummingbird in a similar way, as the flying one shares the harmonious energy of butterflies and dragonflies. If a hummingbird comes to you in a vision, it often represents the need for more laughter and joy in your life. The hummingbird energy suggests that we need to savour the beauty of life and draw upon the bird energy to help create inner peace.

Within the *White Eagle Medicine Wheel* workshop there is an animal journey whereby people are able to connect with their animal guide or totem animal for that period of time. The journey involves spiritual preparation and a willingness to allow energy to blend with the four leggeds, flying, swimming and crawling ones.

Totem Animal Journey

The journey needs to take place in a quiet, peaceful room with good ener-gies. The room must be smudged with sacred sage, cleansing and purifying the atmosphere (as illustrated in Chapter 1). For the Totem Animal Journey, it is advisable to chew a small piece of osha (a herbal medicine root that has been obtained through prayer and permission from the osha root to be utilized). As you chew the osha, pray for a good Totem Animal Journey and spiritual enlightenment. Continue to chew the osha until your journey is complete. Once the sage is burning and the osha becomes soft in your mouth, you are ready to honour the four directions.

Place the tobacco in a sun-wise, clockwise direction, honouring the four directions. Again, begin with the direction that talks to your energy. Make the sacred tobacco circle wide enough to lie your body inside. The last preparation for your journey is to place a crystal or any small, sacred object or artefact of your choice at the top of your head.

Breathe in the scent of the cleansing sage smoke. Taste the osha in your mouth and at the back of your throat. Relax into the sacred smell and taste, breathing deeply and easily. When you are completely at one with your own breathing, allow the sage's smoke dancers to drift into your spirit until you feel more relaxed than you have ever felt before. Keep your eyes closed and use your energy force to look deep within yourself until you see at the innermost centre of your chest, a pinpoint of pale yel-low light.

As you look closer, you will see that the light turns to a bright yellow, like the colour of the sun. Watch the light grow brighter and larger, until it opens up its heart like a flower. Out of this flower, an animal will come. It can be any one of the four leggeds, flying, swimming or crawling ones. The energy you require will come to you naturally. Do not be afraid. Allow your spirit to go with the animal energy. It will take you and you must follow with trust and love in your heart. Release all fear and inner blocks and become one with the Energy Source as you journey to another plane.

After you have completed your journey with your animal spirit, try to remember each detail before the ceremony is concluded. Return to the open flower in your chest and go inside until the flower closes and you can only see the pale yellow light again.

Allow the light to fade slowly and make your way back in your own time to consciousness. Write down your animal journey. If you do not understand it, ask a spiritual adviser or medicine person to help interpret it for you. To make the language of this visionary journey easier, I will share a selection of Totem Animal Journeys people have taken in the *White Eagle Medicine Wheel* workshops.

◄

I will begin with a man who felt unsettled by his journey. Eagle Flies said, 'As the flower in my chest opened, a large, golden eagle flew out.

'As the eagle flew, I flew with it, without words. Suddenly, but smoothly, I became the eagle and flew through the clouds. I swooped over tall, grey buildings until I had flown for many miles.

'I had covered over two thousand miles to return to my country, the land of my birth. I did not go to my home, but to a cliff-top near my house. I circled the high, iron-grey cliff many times.

'The wind blew fiercely in from the sea. The world looked grey and steely blue, but I did not want to fly away. The wind was picking up and I knew I must fly westwards and quickly. I also knew that I would never return or see my birth land again.

'I flew away until the night became pitch black, but I could not stop, I was driven, although I felt cold and lonely. My wings were tired and dirty from the long, weary journey. Then I saw neon city lights and I could hear the awful din of too many people, buildings, machines and vehicles welded together. I looked behind me, but there was only blackness. I could not go back. I knew I had no choice other than to embrace the urban world. This was where I had to land. I was pulled by destiny, although my heart was heavy with pain for what I had lost.' The man was silent.

I asked him why he had left the country where he was raised. He said, 'I wanted adventure, but that strange and desolate island has stayed in my blood. I hardly visit the island any more because all my family moved away years ago. Sometimes, I wish it wouldn't, but the island still comes to me in dreams all the time.'

Eagle Flies looked sad as he spoke. 'What do you think the eagle was trying to show you?' I asked. 'To leave it all behind, I suppose. To accept my life or, at least, understand that my life lies in the big city,' he replied. I said, 'You do not live in that land any longer, but it lives in you. You can fly there any time you want as an eagle. We all return to our birth-place, again and again, our original energy is there. The eagle helped you to see that your energy could fly, there is great power in that, take the freedom of the eagle's wings.

'Your human family may not live there, but what of the land itself, the sitting ones, the rocks, the standing people, the trees, the cliffs and the sea that surround Mother Earth, are all of these not your family as well? Eagle Flies did not respond at first, then he said, 'I have already travelled to many parts of this planet and yet I know there are more physical journeys I must take. I understand that my destiny lies far across these waters. I was looking to the past, now I must look towards the future.'

Eagle Flies asked me, 'Will I become an eagle again when I go on another animal journey?' I responded, 'You have connected with the eagle's energy. If you want to take an animal journey as an eagle again, ask the eagle inside you to fly. If you want to meet one of the many other animals that wish to help you, then you will be taken on a different journey. Trust and go with the rhythm, the four leggeds, flying, swimming and crawling ones will do the rest.'

◄

Crocodile Friend could not stop laughing after she had completed her Totem Animal Journey. Many people joined in her infectious mirth, but they did not know why they were laughing. I asked her what had amused her so much and she could hardly get the words out. Eventually, Crocodile Friend was able to tell me, 'I was terrified at first and did not want the flower to open, because I sensed something odd was going to happen and it certainly did. A crocodile tried to poke its large, slimy, brown-green head into the flower. I screamed at it to go away, but it would not. It was one persistent crocodile. In the end, it wore me down, so I went with it.

'It was the strangest thing, he — I knew it was a male by this time, just by instinct — walked slowly, but steadily ahead of me, looking behind him every so often to make sure I was following. I could not help thinking, I bet I am the only one who ended up with a crocodile.

'The crocodile led me to this river, his home I guess. Then, he sat down on the river-bank and never made a sound or even looked at me. I could tell he was waiting for me to sit down beside him. I still felt a little nervous, but I sat down anyway. We just sat side by side. I wished that he would make a connection with me or do something, but he just sat there quietly.

'I looked at him discreetly out of the corner of my eye. I have to admit I still felt a bit afraid, but curiosity was starting to get the better of me. I noticed the crocodile was extremely old. His leathery skin had lost its colour on the back of his head and there were a few bald patches on his face. In spite of how I feel about crocodiles, I was impressed by his confidence and I could not help but notice the ancient wisdom in his eyes. There were millions of years of knowledge in those mysterious, aeons-old eyes.

'The crocodile turned his old head towards me, leaning it quizzically to one side. Then he gently rubbed the top part of his head against my cheek. I almost felt like hugging him, but he got up and went into the water, only looking back once before disappearing downstream.

'I felt sad that he had gone and wished I had had the nerve to talk to him. I heard a voice, it sounded far away and it said to say goodbye to the animal energy and return to the flower-light. I searched the river, hoping the crocodile would return so I could say goodbye, but he did not return. I shouted, "Goodbye, see you again, I hope."

'As I began my journey back, I suddenly started to laugh at my own silly

fears. The crocodile came in peace to give me some of his age-old wisdom and I was too frightened to take it and that is the story of my life.'

Everyone in the workshop laughed again with Crocodile Friend. She said, 'I think it is pretty clear that I need to learn not to be so fearful.' 'Yes, and to know that wisdom and help can come in any shape or size,' I added. The crocodile wanted the woman to understand there was no need to fear him. He may also have wanted to tell her something, impart some knowledge, but might have felt she needed to get used to him first of all as a friend. I said I believed the old crocodile would come again. Crocodile Friend laughed, 'Next time, I won't be afraid of him. I am sure he wanted to tell me something, but I was too scared to hear. I still can't get over what a kindly old gentleman he was.'

◄

Low Elk held a totem eagle pendant in her hand. She looked at the eagle as she spoke, 'I wondered if the spotted eagle would come. I know the Native American legend about the spotted eagle flying higher than any other bird and that is believed to bring him closer to the Creator. The legend says the closer you get to the Creator, the more likely it is that your prayers will be heard. The eagle's colourful wings also represent the sun, another symbol of close proximity to the Creator. I wanted the golden eagle to be my spiritual guide, but the elk came instead.

'I immediately felt as though the elk was my protector as well as a teacher. The elk made a low, grunting noise in his throat, when he looked at me. The elk moved forward and I followed; although the elk's movements were quick, it was not an effort for me to keep up. The elk started to run and I ran as well. We passed long, windy rivers that were almost dry in the height of summer.

'The sun was extremely hot and I felt as though we were about to enter the fire. The sun had become the fire. I felt a new reverence for nature. As we progressed, I could read the landmarks as spiritual divinations provided by nature.

'The elk ran faster and I lost sight of its swaying antlers. Then he reappeared and hot steam shot out of his nostrils as sweat ran off his body. The elk suddenly buckled under his own weight and lay panting upon the ground. I felt alarmed and afraid. I thought he was dying. I knelt down beside him and laid my hand upon his saturated back. In one quick movement, the elk twisted his head towards me and his sweat shot out and covered my face. I wiped my face and as I did this the elk disappeared. He just vanished. My hand dropped to the ground where he lay and a puddle of his sweat was all that was left.

'Then, I heard a hiss and a rattle and I felt alarmed that there might be a dangerous snake nearby. Nervously, I managed to steal a look behind me to where I heard the noise and I saw an elk horn rattle. I picked up the rattle and understood that this was a gift from the elk. As my spirit-energy returned to this state of being, I felt certain that I needed to use a rattle as part of my own healing process.'

Low Elk did not feel disappointed that the eagle was not her guide on the Totem Animal Journey. Clearly, the elk had given her the vision she was seeking and the knowledge she required.

◄

Flying Hawk Man was taken on a mysterious animal vision journey by a muskrat. Many Native American nations consider the muskrat sacred, and the four legged is placed high upon the totem pole. Flying Hawk Man said, 'I saw a bright-eyed muskrat sitting on top of a medicine lodge. The muskrat backed away and as she retreated a mask fell towards me. I picked up the hawk-mask and fitted it over my face. My own human face seemed to fall away only to be replaced by a smaller head.

'I could see out through the eye-holes of the mask and my view was aerial. I sucked air into my lungs, but my body responded in a different way. My arms did not move, yet they felt outstretched. Although the metaphysical changes were incredible, there was a subtlety that I cannot easily define.

'The spirit of the hawk formed inside my own energy, but it was the hawk that was leading and I was following. The hawk-mask felt tighter around my face and then it interconnected and the mask became the living hawk-face. At the same time, my spirit lost its human complexity and I was the hawk.

'The hawk's life and spirit were expressed in his eyes, wings and claws. My hawk world touched the essence of the sky and the earth, supported by forces derived from the spiritual world. This is what I understood in my hawk-state.

'I could see a medicine lodge in the distance like a shiny, dark pin held between sweetgrass and trees. I flew towards the lodge and dancers leapt high in the air. Their bodies were covered in hawk feathers. They also wore hawk-masks over their faces. The dancers were calling for the guardian spirit of the hawk.

'They sought the hawk's energy. As I flew closer, they removed the hawk-masks and chanted as they pointed excitedly towards the sky. The sky was cloudless, but as their chant rose, a sky-full of hawks flapped strange designs across the sky's broad canvas. The dancers stopped chanting and they did not dance or even move again.

'The hawks became one and I was part of their collective eyes, wings and beaks. The vitality of the enormous hawk-group generated such electricity that we were taken past nature into a celestial light where we dispersed, yet remained together, bathed in a cooling, green light. It was peaceful and silent.

'I slowly returned my spirit to this room, but as I came back I felt the hawk's wings beating inside me. I believe the hawk is my totem bird and protector for this part of my life. It's strange, but now, I cannot imagine my life without the hawk's spirit after my visionary flight.'

The hawk's energy can be called at any time and the energy of the hawks' ancestors. Flying Hawk Man made a profound energy connection with the hawk that will no doubt continue to help him upon his Mother Earth pathway.

◄

Spotted Horse found it difficult to relax long enough to be able to laugh and enjoy life. Spotted Horse took life seriously and felt irritated by those who joked a lot because he considered them irresponsible. This is what his mind told him, but his energy sent a different wisdom to his heart and he realized he had lost an essential part of life; his sense of humour. His vision journey took him past his mind-set to a wonderful plane where he had to learn to laugh.

Spotted Horse smiled, 'As my spirit drifted out of this body, my major concern was to go on the vision and do it correctly.' He was later to learn that there is no correct way of going upon a vision, it is simply a connection to the Energy Source. Energy connection can be reached in many different ways and the Totem Animal Journey is one of the ways that worked for Spotted Horse.

At the beginning of the workshop, Spotted Horse also worried about the amount of time it would take to go upon the vision. As the sacred sage burned, Spotted Horse began to journey into the animal-energy and his spirit lightened as his anxiety disappeared. Spotted Horse said, 'At first, I found it really hard to envision a yellow light or anything. I am not sure if I even managed to see it or not, but somehow, a black and white horse came and stood in front of me. It was literally half-black and half-white. I am afraid of horses and did not want to go anywhere near him. Then the horse's nostrils flared and he kept rearing onto his hind legs and that scared me even more.

'This wild creature cantered around, showing the whites of his eyes and jerking his head until his black and white mane flew in the air. I know I would never have worked up the courage to go with him, but then without any effort on my part, I was, alarmingly, sat on his back. I cannot explain how this happened. I have no memory whatsoever of getting up on his back. As soon as I was sat on his back, he raced off like a motorbike, only I had no control! I was terrified and hung onto his mane like a drowning man.

'The horse galloped harder and harder, then stopped and I flew straight off, over his ears. I landed with quite a bump on the ground, but oddly enough, I was not hurt. The strange horse looked at me and nuzzled my hair. I just sat there hoping he would go away. Then the wild horse jumped up in the air and did what I can only describe as equine-acrobatics. His body contorted almost out of shape and it looked so comical, I forgot my fear and started laughing. I laughed until my sides ached.

'The horse looked as though he was laughing as well. The horse nuzzled my head one last time and then galloped away. Dust rose as his hooves hit the ground and my spirit became part of the dust, until it dissolved into it and I came back to this space and time.'

Spotted Horse's eyes were filled with merriment as I asked him what he believed he had learnt from his four-legged friend. He replied, 'I think I was taking life much too seriously. I was trapped in financial worries and other material concerns. I forgot how to laugh and have fun. I also feel I went through a rebirth of sorts, as my spirit mingled with the dust. I certainly feel different, much lighter. I am going to have to remember how to keep laughing or I will just have to take another horse ride and I am not sure that my stomach is up to it.'

In accordance with Native American beliefs, the black and white horse also represents the medicine horse. It is said that when the black and white medicine horse returns it will have an eagle upon its chest. The appearance of the spiritual eagle-crested black and white horse has been foretold since ancient times.

The Ojibway, the Sioux, the Cherokee, the Apache and Cree nations believe that when this divine horse appears, peace and harmony will be restored to Mother Earth. The medicine horse had already, evidently, helped to restore harmony and humour within Spotted Horse.

Sea Woman told me that her journey left her mystified, but intrigued. During her Totem Animal Journey, Sea Woman was confronted with the power of the sea-energy. Sea Woman said, 'I stood beside the sea with a friend. The sea was almost black-red with fury as she hurled and twisted. I felt the sharp, cold, salt spray cut against my face as the outraged sea whipped over the sea-wall. I turned to my friend, but he did not respond, he was mesmerized by the sea's dark fury. I saw the hulk of a giant ship, just the wooden skeleton as she was battered against the demonic waves. The sea opened its mouth wider and swallowed the ship's frame. The figurehead was devoured first and then the rest of the ship's bones were eaten until only a broken mast remained visible. The ship was pulverized as her will weakened against the might of the sea. I could feel the pain of the ship as she ended her hopeless fight.

'I turned to my friend. His eyes softened, before he lifted me bodily off the ground. I was seized by panic, but my friend smiled kindly as he placed me onto the drowning, splintered mast. I hung onto the mast and then almost immediately, it transformed into a gigantic lizard. The lizard crashed about in the sea and I clung mute with fear upon its back.

'The massive lizard leapt over the sea-wall and raced towards a hilly, green field. I held onto the lizard's scaly neck and then I felt the leathered skin change into coarse, long hair. The lizard had metamorphosed into a silver-white horse. The horse's body shivered as he galloped uphill. I leant forward and allowed myself to become one with the horse's energy. When we reached the summit of the hill, I slipped off the horse's back. The horse looked at me and then disappeared into a rock. I was too stunned to react.'

Sea Woman looked concerned as her story came to a close, 'I do not know what you make of that, but it was one of the strangest experiences I have ever had.' Sea Woman sat back and looked exhausted from her journey. I smiled, 'What do you think the animals shape-shifting meant?' She shook her head, 'I have no idea. I was not afraid of the lizard particularly, although in real life, I have a morbid fear of all reptilian creatures. I felt the horse was highly strung, excitable and that made me uneasy at first, until I was able to unite with the horse's energy.' I asked her what she felt the ship symbolized and she responded, 'The ship, well, the skeleton of a ship, had lost its power. It was dying, almost dead, maybe that means the end of a way

of life or a change of direction in my own life? The lizard could represent new life as the ship changed into one. When I think about the horse, I am aware of the speed and certainty of its direction. I do not know why it would disappear into a rock, but I suppose energy can go wherever it chooses.'

I felt that Sea Woman had understood her journey well. She was able to travel within and interconnect on many different energy levels. The energy took the forms and shapes the woman needed in order to understand their message. At the end of her vision, Sea Woman was left to stand alone on her own two feet. She had reached the top of the hill, a hill-high view of her own life. A hilltop is a good place to observe life all around and embrace the Energy Source.

◄

Bear Running Deer felt his energy drawn away as soon as the Totem Animal Journey began. Bear Running Deer related his visionary journey, 'I left the room almost immediately, that is to say my spirit and energy left the room and I was sheltered by trees. I felt strange, outside my body, yet more inside it than I had ever felt before. I was on the ground, then I stood up. As I stood, I realized I had become a four legged and reared in the air as a towering, black bear. I was totally connected to the freedom of the wilderness. My bear life was cast in forests without any recognition of the world that lay beyond it. The strength within me erupted and my power could crush, but I only wanted to amble in my wooded domain.

'Then in a split second without any warning, I was standing on a triangular-shaped, leafy island. In stark contrast with my bear confidence, I trembled with fear through the eyes of a victim. I was inside the shaking heart of a scorched-red deer. I was startled and terrified by the slightest sound or movement in the long grass. My energy was coiled like a wire in my long, reed-thin legs. I valued my legs above all else, as they were my only means of escape.

'I flexed my legs and made ready for the perpetual flight that epitomized my life as a deer. The grass in my mouth changed to the taste of sage. Then

I smelt the sage burning, and with some relief, I came back to my own body and human form.'

Bear Running Deer took a deep breath. I asked him, 'What have the four leggeds given to you?' He thought for a few seconds, 'The experience of just being a four legged was in itself a gift. It was totally different from being a two legged. When I was a bear, I held the world in my large paw, but the deer was trapped in fear. They gave me an insight into their energy, their way of being that I could never have hoped to understand otherwise.' Bear Running Deer's vision had also shown him the intense strength and vulnerability within himself. It was time he learned to balance those energies in order to make the most of his strength and sensitivity.

I asked Bear Running Deer and all the two leggeds who had participated in the Totem Animal Journey to offer a pinch of tobacco that night and offer thanks. I advised them that the energy connection had been made. The animal connection would continue as long as they allowed their spiritual connection to flow through with their own energy.

However they present themselves, the four leggeds symbolize balance and harmony. There are many more ways to connect with the power of animal energies. As the Totem Animal Journey demonstrates, you can call upon the energies of the four leggeds, flying, swimming and crawling ones, but you can also call upon the energies of all their ancestors. Their powerful energy will teach you what many human beings have forgotten.

Visions given by the Creator often take us to the spirit of the animal energies. The Great Grandfather Spirit beckoned my energy towards White Buffalo calf one night on Turtle Island.

The Legend
of the
Buttala Bay

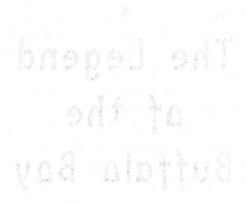

Wash me, for but one word has—forgotten
Upon my people for centuries untold
And that which to us appears meaningless and dumb
May change

SEATTLE — SUQUAMISH

◀

3

The Legend of the Buffalo Boy

Yonder sky that has wept tears of compassion
Upon my people for centuries untold,
And that which to us appears changeless and eternal,
May change.

SEATTLE — SUQUAMISH

I was travelling towards the close of the day across the open prairies in Wyoming. It was a desolate place to man's eye, yet when I looked again, there were spirals of energies circling in the fading sun. I slept in an old western-style hotel that night. The night was warm and the sky was alive with the light of the stars. I settled into bed and had no sooner closed my eyes than the Great Grandfather Spirit was with me. He carried a white baby buffalo calf in his arms. I asked the Great Grandfather Spirit, 'Why have you brought our four-legged friend?' The Great Grandfather Spirit stroked the buffalo's woolly head and said, 'The time is approaching for the white buffalo calf to return again.'

The white buffalo's liquid, soft-brown eyes stared up at me. The Great Grandfather Spirit set the white buffalo upon its feet. The buffalo remained quietly by the Elder's side. The Great Grandfather Spirit sat upon the ground, cross-legged, beside his small, white friend. The buffalo laid his head upon the old man's lap. The Great Grandfather Spirit said, 'There was once a land of buffalo on Turtle Island and the four legged were honoured. Those days have changed so much, it is not possible to recognize Turtle Island any more.

'I took my great grandson to where buffalo had been as plentiful as wild grasses in summer. My young boy wanted to know where they had all gone. I told him, "They were returned to the pure Energy Source where they came from, but Turtle Island continues to mourn their sad loss." '

The Great Grandfather Spirit lowered his head and his tears fell upon the curly, snow-white head. When he spoke again his voice was hoarse with sadness, 'I wonder, when so much was destroyed, why did not even one man raise his head and ask, "Wait my brothers, what will this mean to Mother Earth?" Remember, when a sacred way of life, be it of the four legged or the two legged, is forcibly torn away, then the cut is so deep it runs straight through to the heart of Mother Earth and it takes many, many moons to heal and stop the bleeding.' The white buffalo lifted his head and the Great Grandfather Spirit stood up and walked silently away. The buffalo calf walked beside him and they joined a circle of blue light.

The vision gave way to morning and I woke up. I opened the dark green

shutters and looked out upon the endless prairies. The early light touched the earth. The past felt close and it brought the buffalo. The energy of the four legged thundered on the prairies, although the land was sedate, and I could hear a cricket singing its peculiar song in the wet dew of dawn.

◂

The buffalo is synonymous with the Native American people. The great buffalo lived and passed into spirit with many nations whose names are scattered in the wind and forgotten. The buffalo is still honoured by the Native American people. In the past, they depended upon their four-legged friend for survival and good health. It is believed that the Creator gave the buffalo to the Native American people to ease their burden of hunger and cold. The buffalo provided the two leggeds with food, clothing, shelter and tools.

The buffalo was also used for ceremonial purposes. Every single part of the buffalo was utilized so that nothing was wasted. The skin was used to cover the sacred sweat lodge and tipis. It was also used for blankets and clothing. The intestines were used as sewing thread. The bones were used as digging tools, shaped into cooking tools and they were also utilized as part of certain medicines. The meat was used to feed the people. In the old days, when the buffalo was needed, a ceremony was held to connect with the spirit of the buffalo. In this ceremony, they would dress like their brother, the buffalo, and honour their friend. It is said that when the buffalo heard their message, a vision would be given to the medicine man. In the vision, the medicine man was told where the buffalo would graze, so the next day the hunters would go out and take only what was needed for survival. It was understood that the buffalo was willing to sacrifice its life to help the two legged.

After the hunt was finished, a ceremony would be held to give thanks for what the buffalo had provided. Many Native American nations still perform dances that honour the buffalo. Warriors dance in one direction and the women dance in the opposite direction. This demonstrates a harmonious flow between men and women. It also creates a protective shield for the young and the children dance in the middle.

In the past, when the buffalo was near, it meant abundance and happiness for the Native American nations. It is believed that when buffaloes came in visions and pawed the ground, it was a warning that danger was imminent.

Before the west was lost and the wars fought, many Native Americans said that the spirit of the buffalo had told them that the deceit and greed of the newcomer would destroy many nations. There is a proverb amongst the Native Americans, which says that, 'as long as the buffalo walks upon Mother Earth, so will the two leggeds, but once the buffalo is destroyed, our own end has been foreseen.' The buffalo was destroyed and the free life of the Native American people followed its bloody path. It took less than ten years for the white two leggeds to completely obliterate hundreds of buffalo herds.

The buffalo were slain and the people starved. The buffalo was not only a provider of food and clothing, but the buffalo symbolized spiritual connection and harmony. There are many stories about how the Creator, the Great Spirit, gave the buffalo as a gift to the Native American people.

Although, there are variations of the white buffalo calf myth, the essence of the myths is the same, whereby the white buffalo calf is recognized as the most sacred buffalo calf. In accordance with the myths, all others buffaloes were given permission to walk upon Mother Earth by the birth of the white buffalo calf. The Blackfoot nation's white buffalo calf myth begins in the most sacred of all places, the Spirit World.

THE BLACKFOOT WHITE BUFFALO CALF MYTH

The Spirit World was willing to make a great sacrifice and send a rare and beautiful energy to Mother Earth to help her people. They saw that many people were suffering from the freezing winter months with little food to feed them. This touched the heart of the Spirit World and a spiritual Council was held that lasted for many days.

At last, they placed their hands together, joining their energy, and a white buffalo calf came into being. They had created the energy and knew it would find its way into the form that was needed. They joined hands again and the energy dispersed as the pact had been sealed.

The Necklace Chief, Ninaa, of the Spirit World sent word to the rest of the Energies, saying that one of their Elders of the spirit world would be selected to be born into the world of the flesh; the human race. Ninaa said they must help an Elder decide to become a man-child and join the human race, the two leggeds upon Mother Earth. It was considered a great honour to go to this green and blue world, although, in their hearts, many were sad at the thought of leaving the safe, white light and protection of the Spirit World. Mother Earth was shown in energy form and something stirred in another life energy. This energy would be known later as the Buffalo Boy.

The spiritual Elders gathered in a great Council in the Creator's Lodge. Within that sacred Lodge the great grandparents and grandparents of all creation sat together. These spiritual great grandparents and grandparents were there to help the Energies choose out of the many who had volunteered to become a two legged. The mission of the chosen energy was to protect and nourish Mother Earth and her people. After many days of telepathic and verbal discussion an understanding was felt and the energy rose. They looked towards a particular energy form and named him the Buffalo Boy. The Buffalo Boy's compassion melted into the new alignment of energy and so he was transformed.

The Buffalo Boy's energy glowed blue as his energy spun in the direction of human life, but darkness also fell about its edges. For one blood-stained instant, the Buffalo Boy energy's felt the diabolical carnage that would befall the people whose energy he would share. Then the energy moved again and it was light once more. The Buffalo Boy knew that in spite of the treachery and decimation of the Native American way of life, somewhere in the expansive and changeable moods of time, the Old Ways would return. The Buffalo Boy smiled and tears fell down his cheeks before they turned into sky-blue ponds.

The Council helped to prepare the Buffalo Boy for his journey and new life as a male human being. The Great Council gave instructions about what was to be achieved once adulthood was reached. Sacred guardians were assigned to watch over the energy of the Buffalo Boy. In order to travel to Mother Earth as a human being, it was essential that only certain gifts were taken and memories selected for human life. There was also the important task of selecting human parents to look after the chosen one, although it was understood he would only be with them as long as their energy combination was necessary. After much discussion, an old man and woman were elected for this honour. This old couple had much wisdom and would be able to teach the chosen Elder, the Buffalo Boy, all he would need to know as a human being and as a young child.

The old couple were the poorest of all the poor tribes. They were of a people known as the Nitsotaapi, which means Real People. The man's name was Sikatisis which translates as Black Leggings. His wife was called Otaikimmio'Tokaan Aakii or Golden Eagle Woman. This couple had been married for over twenty winters and although they prayed and offered kinnick kinnick, they were still childless. Kinnick kinnick is the red bark scraped off the willow tree that the Nitsotaapi used in the sacred channupa (pipe) to pray to the Great Spirit. The old couple's prayers went unanswered; that is, until the moment of the energy connection. They were to learn that energy connection is often made when you least expect it.

That night as Sikatisis lay sleeping his energy was called upon the vision plane. First he saw blue-black hills thundering towards him. As the galloping hills came closer, his heart beat faster. Sikatisis saw that they were not hills at all, but thousands of buffaloes. Sikatisis became afraid and believed he would be trampled, but as they raced closer, they swerved and galloped ever faster away. When the dust cleared, there was one little white buffalo calf left. The buffalo calf stared into Sikatisis' eyes until their energies touched. Sikatisis began to shake with fear and happiness.

Sikatisis woke up and held his wife tight. Otaikimmio'Tokaan Aakii whispered, 'My husband, I am ready for you.' Sikatisis believed his wife had entered his vision too and understood, as he did, that they were to

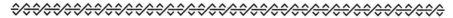

have a child. They made love. They danced the dance of life as they had never done before.

Afterwards, as they lay cradled together, Sikatisis said, 'We are not young, but there is much the young do not have that we have, my good woman, my good wife.' Otaikimmio'Tokaan Aakii smiled in the darkness and caressed her husband's arm and she felt the love of all the years they had spent together filling her heart with a warm glow.

'We will have a child my love, my good man, my good husband.' Sikatisis' old eyes filled with tears and he held Otaikimmio'Tokaan Aakii even tighter, 'Our baby is coming and he begins to grow under your heart in your kind, soft body tonight.' Then they slowly got up and wrapped a blanket around one another and walked as one outside their tipi in the coolness of the dark night. They placed kinnick kinnick upon the earth, to the four directions, honouring Mother Earth and Grandfather Sky. They were offering thanks, as they knew their prayers had already been heard.

The Nitsotaapi village looked in shock and disbelief as they saw Otaikimmio'Tokaan Aakii's belly grow. The women saw the way Otaikimmio'Tokaan Aakii smiled to herself and rubbed her stomach. They saw the way she looked at Sikatisis and how they laughed quietly to each other as Sikatisis fussed over his wife. He would not allow her to do any hard work. This was not the way of the Nitsotaapi people, as women worked hard, and being with child made no difference. This was not a secret to be kept, yet the old couple did not want to share their baby, not just yet. Let the tribe celebrate with them when the child was born.

Meanwhile, the Buffalo Boy was asked by the spiritual great grandparents to close his eyes and sing a sacred song. The Buffalo Boy did as he was asked and when the song was finished, he was inside Otaikimmio'Tokaan Aakii's body; warm and safe. It was snowy mid-winter by the time Otaikimmio'Tokaan Aakii's tipi was filled with skilled medicine women.

The medicine women had been watching her closely for days and knew she was ready to give birth. The tribe felt compassion and friendship for Otaikimmio'Tokaan Aakii and Sikatisis. They were worried the strain of a first child to such an old woman might kill her or the baby, or both. It was the middle of the night when the baby was born and there was great excitement in the village.

Otaikimmio'Tokaan Aakii's baby slipped into the world easily and cried out as his little body hit the cold, night air. There was awe and talk amongst the tribe of spiritual intervention, how else could such a birth have taken place? The women were mystified about how easily Otaikimmio'Tokaan Aakii gave birth without even one scream. The tribe's Chief listened and nodded as his people spoke of the wondrous birth, but the Chief said nothing, because he understood the Creator had helped the aged couple.

Although the tribe did not have many rich gifts to give, the Chief gave his best buffalo hide to this new-born baby. Sikatisis smiled with his secret knowledge as he accepted the buffalo hide and thanked the Nitsotaapi Chief. Sikatisis said he would name his child Buffalo Boy.

The Nitsotaapi Chief felt honoured and he believed that the child was named Buffalo Boy because of the gift he had given him. The Chief was so pleased, Sikatisis did not have the heart to tell him about his buffalo vision. Apart from that, Sikatisis understood energy and knew that we are all related, and everything is interwoven between all living things.

It cannot be forgotten that Sikatisis and Otaikimmio'Tokaan Aakii, despite their great joy, were old. The Nitsotaapi Chief and the rest of the tribe gathered in a Council to decide how best to help the proud new parents, who were really the age of grandparents. Soon it was decided that the young warriors would hunt for the family and the women would bring them wood for their fire.

This settled, Sikatisis and Otaikimmio'Tokaan Aakii set about raising their Buffalo Boy baby. The moons changed quickly, as they do with children. The boy was already four years old when Sikatisis was tying the last of his belongings onto the third dog. All the Nitsotaapi tribe went to better hunting grounds in the winter. They followed the buffalo.

Sikatisis' young son, the Buffalo Boy, sat playfully on the travois, a wooden and animal skin covered stretcher pulled by dog to transport the family's belongings. Then the Buffalo Boy climbed upon the broad, strong back of the large, grey dog attached to the travois. Suddenly, the dog jerked

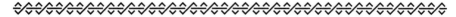

forward and ran away with the boy. Sikatisis shouted after the dog, but he did not stop.

Otaikimmio'Tokaan Aakii heard the noise and came out of her tipi just in time to see her precious son disappear over a small hill. Otaikimmio'-Tokaan Aakii screamed and the tribe, who were preparing their own belongings for a new camp, came running over to the trembling couple.

Sikatisis told them what had happened and the Chief arranged a large search party. The Chief said, 'We cannot move from this camp until the Buffalo Boy is found.' They searched all day and all night, even the women and children searched, but they could not find the Buffalo Boy. They searched and searched, but there was no sign of the Buffalo Boy and each day the tribe saw Sikatisis' and Otaikimmio'Tokaan Aakii's hearts and spirits become heavier. The Nitsotaapi Chief could not risk his people any longer. The days were too cold and food was running out.

After the fourth day the Chief called a Council and placed Sikatisis and Otaikimmio'Tokaan Aakii at the centre of the circle, 'My people, I have spoken to the Great Spirit. I have asked for his help and made many offerings, as I know you all have. Yet, the Buffalo Boy has not been found. He may even be with the Great Spirit as we speak. If this is so, there is no need for tears because he will be in a place of no hunger, cold or pain.'

When the Chief finished, all the tribe cast their eyes upon the floor because they did not want to see the pain in the faces of Sikatisis and Otaikimmio'Tokaan Aakii. The old couple just held each other's hands tightly and Sikatisis spoke for them, 'I do not know why we have lost the greatest gift Gitchgee Manito ever gave us. I will pray, I will fast, I will make offerings and do many ceremonies until one day, I know my little son will return to Otaikimmio'Tokaan Aakii and me.'

The Council drew to a close and the heart-weary tribe moved on. Sikatisis and Otaikimmio'Tokaan Aakii remained at the back of the camp and every so often you could hear the old woman's quiet weeping. You could also see Sikatisis looking hopefully behind him.

The energy forces combined together so that the Buffalo Boy would be led to a place of great learning. He was taken to where he needed to be, but the parting was abrupt and frightening for the young boy. The large dog was young and eager and he had boundless energy.

The dog ran so fast that the cactus caught the travois and it was pulled straight off his back, but the boy did not dare to look back or let go of the dog's neck. The dog headed east and ran for two days and two nights. Eventually, the Buffalo Boy was so exhausted that he had to let go of the dog's hair. The Buffalo Boy fell to the ground with a thud and landed in a strange, new place. It was the Buffalo tribe's winter camping ground. The Buffalo Boy was so shocked by what had happened, he just sat dazed, holding his bleeding temple with his tired hands.

The Buffalo tribe was not an ordinary tribe, they had a similar energy to the small boy, although they did not recognize this at first. Memory, time and space are different in the Spirit World. Much is forgotten so that an earth life is lived without wishing to return home to the pure Energy Source.

The Buffalo tribe's women were bathing themselves in the river when they heard a noise and saw a big, grey dog running wildly. Then, something fell off the dog's back. The women dried themselves quickly and went to investigate. They were enchanted with the little boy they found and picked him up. One woman held him close to her and the Buffalo Boy's energy was revived.

The women took the young boy to the Buffalo Chief. The Buffalo Chief laughed loudly when he heard the story. He wiped tears of laughter from his eyes and said, 'So we must call him Mad Dog Boy.' The young boy knew that was not right, and he spoke with confidence, 'I already have a name, I am called the Buffalo Boy.' When he said this, he looked the Chief straight in his black-brown eyes without flinching.

This was something most young boys would be afraid to do as it was considered disrespectful. As they looked into each other's eyes, time fell away and old memories from another place took them to the birth home: the Spirit World.

Their energies circled together. All the buffalo tribe had gathered and watched in amazement as the Buffalo Chief swayed from side to side as if in a vision or a trance and the little boy did the same. It seemed like a long

time as we understand time, yet it was not such a long time before the Chief shook his head and steadied himself and the Buffalo Boy also stood still.

The Buffalo Chief spoke, 'Now I understand why you were sent to me and my tribe. Your energy is similar to ours. You have been sent by the Spirit World to help the human race. Do you know what is up ahead for the two leggeds unless they learn the lesson of true compassion, forgiveness and peace?'

The Buffalo Boy shook his head. The Chief looked at the boy and then at all his people and back to the little boy as he spoke again, 'There will be terrible wars, starvation and diseases we have never even heard of before. They will come from far away, across the seas and these people from across the sea will carry merciless weapons that the people of this country, Turtle Island, have never even seen before. The people who come from across the sea will take the life of every last buffalo and leave us to starve in the winter.

They will rip the earth open and desecrate the forest until not one tree is left standing and only the bleached bones of human and animal life will be left drying in the sun. Even Father Sun, my Buffalo Boy, towards the end of earth time as we know it, will become so hot that it will scorch the skin of all those few pitiful ones left living. This will happen and worse, if the attacks upon Mother Earth and all living things are not prevented.'

The Buffalo Boy was not able to speak at first and then he asked, 'How can we stop these terrible things?' The Chief replied, 'It is not for us to stop them because we are at peace with Mother Earth, it is for those who are not, that need to learn. If they understood the energy connection, this would never happen. It will not be stopped, I have seen it in my visions. Father Sun will rage, the skies and seas will roar at what has been done to them. When they have no air left for their lungs because all other life that helped sustain them is gone, they too will return to the Energy Source.'

The Buffalo Boy's young eyes filled with tears as he asked in a low voice, 'What will happen to the men who came and destroyed all living things and Mother Earth?' The Chief held out his hand and touched the young boy's wet face, 'It will be many, many moons before they finally realize what they have done. It will creep up on them. The sign will be the slow seizure of

Mother Earth. Remember, what the two legged poison upon Mother Earth, will in turn poison the two legged.'

The Buffalo Boy hung his head and the Buffalo tribe gathered around him. The Chief touched the young boy's hair, 'Do not cry for them or for us. We come from a much better place and we shall return to the Spirit World, all of those who respect life will return. I know you have lived with a kind, old couple of the earth, I will return you to them when you have spent twelve years in my care. I will teach you all I can and it is my hope and the hope of all living things that those who have eyes, yet are blind, will learn to see and begin to honour all living things as we are all related.'

The Buffalo Boy stayed with the Buffalo tribe until he had reached his sixteenth year. He had learned about universal justice, respect for all living things and how to protect Mother Earth. Compassion was already deeply ingrained in his nature. In his sixteenth year, the Buffalo tribe bade him farewell. They never said goodbye, because they knew they would meet again in their real home, the Spirit World.

The Buffalo tribe placed the young man at the foot of a hill where his human father was fasting and offering prayers and tobacco to the Creator for the safe return of his long-lost son. The Buffalo Boy's heart went out to the crumbling old man whose hair had grown snow white with the passing years.

The Buffalo Boy, a strong, courageous young man by that moon-time, raced up the hill and cried, 'Father, Father, do you not know me? It is your son, the Buffalo Boy.' The old man's sight had become dim with old age and carrying too much sadness. Maybe he did not want to see his own lonely life. He looked at this tall, striking young man with long, shining, black hair. Sikatisis fell to his knees and cried out in pain, 'Do not allow this to be a vision, Creator. I have suffered too much and I have known pain too long. I have lost my wife, my beautiful, good woman, Otaikimmio'Tokaan Aakii, two summers ago and you know how the loss of our son clawed at our tired old hearts. I ask you, do not let this be a vision.' The Buffalo Boy ran over and held his feeble, old father. 'Father, look at me. It is not a vision. I have come back to you. My own heart weeps at the news that my mother is gone to the Spirit World before you, because I know how much you loved her. Believe me father, she is happy, even more than you are at your son's return.' The old man wept until he felt weak with joy and pain. The Buffalo Boy helped him down the hill and after the shock of the boy's return, there was much rejoicing in the Nitsotaapi tribe.

The old Nitsotaapi Chief had recently passed onto the Spirit World and a new Chief had to be selected. Most of the tribe were elderly and ready to pass on to the next level. They were tired and did not want to take on the responsibility of being a Chief. After a short Council it was decided that the strange and enigmatic Buffalo Boy, who was so protected by the Creator and returned to them as a gift, would become their new Chief.

The Buffalo Boy became the Buffalo Boy Chief of the Nitsotaapi tribe. He was a kind and wise leader and the Nitsotaapi tribe was often greatly surprised by his knowledge. They secretly believed he must have gone to the Spirit World, learned great wisdom and had come back to help them. How else could one so young know so much and arrive just when they needed a new Chief? They also remembered his strange, painless birth. They understood that the Energies were working with them.

The Nitsotaapi tribe was peaceful and in harmony with all living things. However, not all neighbouring tribes understood peace. Some tribes camped nearby felt that it would be easy to steal the one horse the Nitsotaapi owned during the night. They also planned to steal blankets for the cold winter. The Buffalo Boy Chief read the bad intention in their hearts. He looked upon them with sadness as they schemed and planned their attack.

One of the neighbouring tribes robbed the Nitsotaapi of their horse and threadbare blankets. The Buffalo Boy Chief's heart was pained by this callous act and he went to speak with the Chief of the thieving tribe. The Buffalo Boy Chief held Councils, one after the other, with many Chiefs of different tribes spread across the land, trying to explain the need for honesty, harmony and peace amongst people. The Buffalo Boy Chief spoke of the earth, but the other Chiefs laughed, 'We already know how to take care of the earth, and why would anyone destroy their own source of life, our mother?'

The Buffalo Boy Chief persisted, 'Men will come from across the sea who do not understand the needs and limitations of Mother Earth's endurance. They will destroy much of what grows upon her back and beneath her waters and above her head.' The Chiefs believed that the young Buffalo Boy Chief's energy had been captured by bad spirits.

They could not comprehend what he was saying, 'Kill all the buffalo? There are more buffalo than grass on the ground. The young Buffalo Boy Chief has been taken over by evil and playful spirits.' This is what they believed and so they continued to war with each other and although they nurtured and protected Mother Earth, they failed to love and protect each other with the same care.

In his twentieth year, the Buffalo Boy Chief had a vision. He saw the big ships landing on Turtle Island, carrying men with killing machines in their hands. The Buffalo Boy Chief knew it was too late and that there was nothing he could do.

The Buffalo Boy Chief said to his father, Sikatisis, 'It is time for you to come with me, my kind old father. I am taking you back to the Spirit World and all the Nitsotaapi tribe will come with us. I have spoken to the people and they have told me they are too old and tired to walk upon the winter grounds any more.' The old man nodded wisely, 'I was hoping I would not have to be parted from you again.' The Buffalo Boy Chief took his father's hand and gathered all the good, old people of the Nitsotaapi tribe and told them to close their eyes and sing a sacred song together. When they opened their eyes, they were in the most beautiful place they had ever seen, the Spirit World, and that is where they chose to stay.

Sikatisis immediately looked for his wife, Otaikimmio'Tokaan Aakii, but he did not have to look far, as she was standing there waiting for him with her arms outstretched. They kissed each other and became youthful again. They held their precious son, the Buffalo Boy, between them and they felt joy as they had never experienced it before. A soft blue light surrounded them as they returned to pure energy and became part of the original Source once more.

On Mother Earth, the men came from across the sea to Turtle Island and

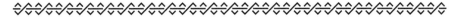

killed many of her people. In a short time, there was only a handful left and their great friends and providers, the buffalo, were slain almost to the last one. The blood of the Native American people and the buffalo mixed together and ran scarlet like a burning river across the subdued prairies.

Even now, many, many years later, if you listen carefully and place your ear against the emptied land when the wind blows, you can still feel their energy and connect with their spirit. On other nights, it is strangely cold and not even the lightest breath of wind blows in the heart of winter. If you walk alone on the cold, desolate prairies and look closely between the sky and the land, you can see the buffalo running wild and free as the wind alongside their friend, the Native American, as their energies remain connected.

◄

The buffalo continues to hold a sacred place within the hearts of the Native American people today. Since ancient times, the Sioux nations have said that when a white buffalo stands upon only three legs, then the end of time upon Mother Earth as we know it is near. I also interpret this omen to signify current scientific, animal experimentation that goes against the natural laws of nature.

Like all energy, if technology and science are used for the good, whilst respecting the natural order, then it can help Mother Earth. Mother Earth's natural balance is paradoxically both fragile and strong. It has already been unhinged by human interference and in time, if we are not careful and do not resolve the problems, the hinge will snap.

On 20 August 1994 a white buffalo calf was born on a farm in Wisconsin. Native American people travelled all across Turtle Island to visit the sacred, promised four legged. The people brought gifts and offered prayers, believing that the white buffalo calf signalled the return of their old, spiritual way of life as well as the buffaloes. The arrival of two more white buffalo calves since has added to the hope that a harmonious life on Mother Earth might be possible once again.

Many people believe the prophecy is coming to pass as there is a pro-gramme to reintroduce the buffalo onto a few selected reservations. 'Wind River Reservation' in South Dakota is one of the chosen lands. This is the express wish of the Native American people and there are further talks of returning more buffaloes to their ancestral lands.

The Native Americans feel the buffalo belongs with their energy. It is a good sight to see the buffaloes running wild and free once again on native lands as the energy from the past, present and future fuses together.

As I said, it was foretold hundreds of years ago by our ancestors that the birth of a white buffalo calf would signal the return of spirituality and ancient balance. This also corresponds with the Lakota Sioux's legend of the White Buffalo Calf Woman.

Similar to the white buffalo calf myths, all Native American nations have their own mythical variations on how the sacred channupa (pipe) was first given to their particular nation. The sacred channupa is a gift to be shared and the myths inform us that the channupa, like all other sacred objects, has a sacred, spiritual origin.

The Lakota Sioux still consider the buffalo sacred above all other four leggeds, and call upon the buffalo energy in ceremonies to help them upon their spiritual pathway. Black Elk, the renowned Oglala Sioux visionary, recounted the legend of the White Buffalo Calf Woman who brought the sacred channupa to the Native American people.

THE LAKOTA SIOUX MYTH OF THE WHITE BUFFALO CALF WOMAN

Black Elk said that two men were out hunting buffalo when they saw a remarkably beautiful woman dressed all in white. One hunter was in awe of the woman and showed her respect through pure thoughts. The second hunter was overcome by his lascivious nature and he wanted to possess her.

The mystical beauty sensed the dark energy in the second hunter's heart and cast a cloud upon him. When the cloud lifted, only the second hunter's bones remained and snakes slid in to where the man once stood. The first hunter fell to his knees and implored the White Buffalo Calf Woman to have mercy upon him and his people. The woman's kindness touched the man as she led him back to his people, the Lakota Sioux.

The White Buffalo Calf Woman gave the sacred channupa to the Lakota Sioux and showed them how to use it, but she warned them that the channupa is sacred and must be honoured at all times. The White Buffalo Calf Woman said that there were four ages in her and that she would watch over the people in every age, and would return to them at the end of the four ages.

It is said that when the White Buffalo Calf Woman returns, there will be peace and prosperity for all upon Mother Earth. Mother Earth herself will also be cleansed and renewed.

Calling the Buffalo Energy

To perform the Buffalo Ceremony, as with all rituals, pure and compassionate feelings in your heart are the key to the strength of the ceremony. The buffalo's energy is honoured as powerful and you must be sure of why you wish to call upon it. It may be simply to exchange energies and understand the buffalo's four-legged life.

Be clear in your ceremonial prayers as the Energies need clarity and simplicity in order to respond. At the beginning of the ceremony, honour the Creator, four directions and the buffalo by offering tobacco and prayers. Sit inside the four directions where the tobacco is laid. You will also need to smudge yourself and the area with sacred sage, providing cleansing and purification.

It is better to conduct this ceremony in an open space like a field or meadow. Ideally, it is preferable to go to where the buffalo once ran free across the prairies on Turtle Island. Their energy is still strong, caught in the grasses and held in the scent of the wild flowers. If you cannot go to Turtle Island, then call the buffalo energy across the sea to you.

You will need some symbolic artefact representing the buffalo. This can be a picture, or you can use a buffalo mask placed over your own face. If you use a picture, then lay it in front of you inside the tobacco circle.

A drum is also required in this ceremony as it represents the thundering feet of the buffalo. Sit upon the ground with a drum on your lap and beat a rhythm that speaks to you. Let the energy of the drum match your own heartbeat. Later the buffalo's energy will join your drum song.

Allow your energy to blend with the buffalo's and feel the largeness of his heart so that your own heart gathers strength. See the buffalo's enormous head reaching to the floor and then lifting as he or she prepares to run. Feel the power and speed as your own legs race with the buffalo. As your energies intertwine, sing a song or chant to honour the buffalo's energy. Sing or chant out loud and do not be afraid to use your voice. Play the drum to keep time and let the buffalo energy grow within you until your energies unite.

When your energy is one magnetic force, speak to the buffalo and ask for the help you require. Be willing to give as you receive. Lay your weight against the buffalo and you will be held upright until you feel ready to stand on your own two feet. Allow yourself to return to your own energy slowly, matching the slower humming energy with a quieter drum-beat and a fainter song or chant. The drumming and chanting will finish at a natural point. Say, 'Mitakuye Oyasin' or 'to all my Relations' before honouring the ancestors of the buffalo with prayers.

Lay your drum to one side and remove your mask if you have been wearing one, and put it on top of the drum. If you used a picture, lay that on top of the drum. Leave the tobacco upon the earth and walk around once in a sun-wise direction before leaving the circle.

The buffalo and the ancestors may come to you in visions after this ceremony. Over time, your understanding and connection to the buffalo energy will grow. Ultimately, this will lead you to a greater understanding of the power of your own inner reserves, determination and ability to walk a truthful pathway.

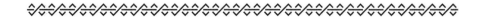

4

Words Carried in the Wind

Now I light the pipe,
And after I have offered it to the powers
That are one Power,
And sent forth a voice to them,
We shall smoke together.

BLACK ELK (1863—1950), OGLALA SIOUX

The green light of new life filled the air and echoed in the canyons. Spring breathed upon Mother Earth and the energy of new life gave rebirth to all living things. I watched the first shy heads of young buds blossom into wild flowers and shine as they gave healing to the world. Sacred, medicinal herbs and plants burst into life and gave fresh protection to Mother Earth and all those who walk upon her. Faint swirls of smoke rose on each hill. The four leggeds felt the energy call and tasted the sweet healing of newly-grown grasses, herbs and plants. The time to journey to Mother Earth had come for them as well. I watched the young foals repeatedly stagger and fall until they finally found their way onto stilt-high legs. I laughed with them as they made their first unsteady, jagged walk. In a short time, they would jump with joy as their energies celebrated the miracle of being alive.

The air was warm and easy to breathe. This was a good time for the four leggeds, flying, swimming and crawling ones to join life upon Mother Earth. The day was settling into twilight, but the gentle heat of the day's sun lent the night-brother some warmth. I was still smiling at the delighted surprise in the young animals' eyes as they took their first steps when I fell into a deep sleep.

The Great Grandfather Spirit came towards me. His hands were clasped in front of him. I noticed there was a light, blue-grey smoke rising on a hill behind him. His great grandson appeared from behind the Elder's back. The young boy smiled at me and pointed towards the rising smoke.

The Great Grandfather Spirit held out one arm and his great grandson slipped his small, brown hand into his Great Grandfather's large, weathered hand. The Elder blew into the air and a wisp of silver-tinged smoke drifted upwards. The Great Grandfather Spirit smiled at his great grandson and squeezed his hand. The Great Grandfather Spirit turned and walked away with his great grandson and I understood that I must follow. The Great Grandfather Spirit and the young boy led me to a tall tipi covered with resplendent animal paintings and symbols.

The Great Grandfather Spirit entered first and the young boy smiled as he held the doorway open for me. The great grandson sat beside his Great

Grandfather. I faced them as we formed a triangular shape. The Great Grandfather Spirit gave me a little water to drink and said, 'There is a special gift coming to you in the next moon. It is your choice whether you want to take this gift or not. Now, you must leave us for a short time and walk alone outside.'

I did as I was asked and went outside. I heard a deep, rumbling sound coming from the east. The noise grew louder and turned into a deep growl. I looked eastwards and saw a large black bear rushing towards me with heavy, thudding feet. My mind instructed me to run, but my spirit insisted that I face the black bear. The bear stopped for a few seconds and exchanged energy by looking into my eyes before it ran away. I understood the energy-message to mean, 'Prepare yourself'. At that moment, a warrior appeared and chased the bear, not as a hunter, but as a playful friend. The warrior stopped running and handed me a sacred bundle, 'This is your gift, if you want it. Take it to the Great Grandfather Spirit and open it.'

I reentered the tipi and placed the bundle upon the ground in front of the Great Grandfather Spirit and the young boy. The bundle was made of fine buckskin leather. The leather was held in place by a purple cloth that formed three crosses. I removed the purple binding and opened the sacred bundle. It revealed the separated long stem and bowl of the sacred pipe. The Great Grandfather Spirit looked at me and then at the pipe. I understood that the energy of the pipe was part of my connection to the Creator and to myself. In time I would be able to assemble its energy inside my own energy.

A vision within my vision flashed before my eyes: it showed the pipe being placed in the middle of a roasting fire. Then I realized that what we see is not always understood and we must look beyond to get the true picture.

I looked up at the Great Grandfather Spirit and I knew he had connected with my energy pattern. 'There is a ceremony you must perform with the sacred channupa. Part of the ceremony honours the fire-energy, but it does not mean you have to burn the channupa.' He laughed and then continued, 'The first thing you must do, my brother, is to dig a hole which should be four inches deep and a little longer than the length of the chan-nupa and stem. Then offer a pinch of tobacco and honour the four direc-tions. Complete this ceremony by putting a little more tobacco in the centre.

'After this, make a bed of sacred sage in the earth-bed. Offer a pinch of tobacco to the sacred channupa bowl itself. Take some more sage and roll it into a ball, mixing your energy with the sacred plant. Connect the bowl and stem together. Light the ball of sage and use the first sacred sage smoke to smudge the channupa. Offer the pipe to the Creator, the four directions, grandfather sky and Mother Earth. Add some sage to the tobacco inside the bowl. Place the channupa into the prepared earth-bed and cover it with sacred sage. You must finish this ceremony by covering the earth-bed with soft clay. Get a bowl of water and place it beside the earth-bed, then build a small fire on top of the sacred covered hole. Light the fire. The four elements are now in your sacred space; earth, water, fire and air.

'Let the fire burn down until there are only chalky ashes left. Leave the channupa safe in Mother Earth overnight to bless it. The Creator and Ener-gies will join Mother Earth and the sacred channupa will be as one by the first light that rises in the sky.

'The next day, you must get a turquoise cloth and sweep the ashes into it. Disconnect the bowl from the stem. Place the bowl in a yellow cloth and the stem in a blue cloth and then put them inside a purple bundle. Tie the bundle with a strip of purple cloth making three crosses. The sacred chan-nupa belongs to you, it is your special gift. Your energies belong together. Smoke the channupa in a sacred way and you will connect with the Energy Source.' A cloud of stone-silver smoke surrounded us and then I awoke.

◂

I had been given permission to carry and smoke the sacred channupa. I had participated in the pipe ceremony many times, but before this vision I had never thought about carrying a pipe. A lot of responsibility comes with being a pipe carrier. If a person carries the sacred channupa, then that per-son cannot have any anger in the heart or energy. If there is anger, then the

pipe must be buried in Mother Earth and not brought to the surface again until the anger is gone.

Anger is a human emotion and sometimes it is necessary. There is powerful energy in anger, and if it can be channelled towards the good, then its energy is fully utilized. Unfortunately, anger often finds a negative outlet in two leggeds.

Shortly after my vision, in the new moon, a man approached me and held a gift in his hands. The man spoke, 'I have been waiting for you. I was told in a vision to make this black pipe and when the spirit was ready, you would come for it. I recognize you from my vision.' I held the black pipe in my hands and thanked the man. The man shook my hand and left.

The sacred black pipe has become an intrinsic part of my energy and I share it with the people in many healing pipe ceremonies. The Sacred Channupa Ceremony offers guidance about being a pipe carrier and performing the sacred channupa ceremony.

Sacred Channupa Ceremony

Many people wish to carry a pipe and perform sacred channupa ceremonies. Yet, it is important to remember that the sacred channupa is connected to the Spirit World and it is better to wait for a vision or to receive direct permission from the Creator before carrying the sacred pipe. If you feel strongly that you need to carry a pipe, then ask the Creator and the Energies to guide you upon that pathway if it is the right one for you. You will be granted permission in a vision or in some other way that you will easily understand if you are to carry a sacred channupa.

As a pipe carrier, there is great spiritual responsibility. I understand and accept that my heart must be free of anger and other negative energy. When I perform the sacred channupa ceremonies, I follow a sacred code in keeping with what the Energies have shown me.

I smudge myself first, then the sacred channupa and the area with sacred sage before I begin the ceremony. Once this is done, I hold the bowl of the sacred pipe with my left hand, which is the hand closest to my heart.

I feel the connection between myself and Mother Earth. I let feelings of love and compassion flow with my own energy. I breathe in cool, refreshing air. Then, I am ready to fill the pipe with sacred tobacco or kinnick kinnick. Kinnick kinnick can also be mixed with osha. The bowl is ready to be filled with tobacco and I attach the stem to the bowl. The bowl represents the woman and the stem symbolizes the man. By joining them together, the natural balance of nature and life is brought together harmoniously.

I am ready to pray. I acknowledge and honour the Creator and the four directions. I begin my prayers in the east, then the south and west and last of all, the north. As I look to the east, I thank the Creator for each new day he has given me and for the lessons and wonders of the rising morning sun. I offer tobacco to Mother Earth.

Then, I turn to the south and smile at the springtime that brings many herbs to heal the sick. Again, I offer tobacco to Mother Earth. I am ready to meet the west, the quiet direction of the orange-red setting sun. The west has given me many vision journeys. On other nights, it has allowed me to lie still and I have rested. Again, I offer tobacco to Mother Earth. Finally, I face the north, the direction that has brought me prophetic visions, battles and warnings, which in time I learned to interpret.

There is a special north language and after many years, I have learned to understand and speak the north tongue. I have made my peace with the north. Once again, I offer more tobacco to Mother Earth.

I look at the beauty of Mother Earth and honour her with words and ask for her permission to let me continue with the sacred pipe ceremony. I thank her for all the ingredients she has provided which now fill the sacred pipe. I look up at grandfather sky and honour him, asking him to help carry my message to the Great Spirit, the Creator. I keep my final and most important offering for the Creator and I thank him for Mother Earth, grandfather sky and the sacred pipe I am about to smoke. I ask him to hear my prayers.

I place a pinch of tobacco upon the ground. I pray from my heart, I say whatever is in my heart and ask for guidance as I pray. There is a Lakota grandfather prayer that you may like to say:

~~~~~~

SACRED LAKOTA PIPE PRAYER

Channupa wan yuha hoye wayinktelo	*I am going to pray with the pipe*
Kola hoye wayinktelo	*My friend I am going to send a voice*
Channupa wan yuha hoye wayinktelo	*I am going to pray with the pipe*
Kola namichikun yelo	*My friend hear me out*

You can repeat this simple, but powerful prayer many times. If there is a group participating in the sacred pipe ceremony, pray together. This will make the energy connection stronger. It will also link your hearts as brothers and sisters.

Look for a moment, and reflect upon past moons. What have you learnt? How have you grown into your own spirit and energy? There is no need for guilt or anger. What is done is done, good or bad, it is simply another lesson learnt. Forgive yourself, forgive others and let the pains that do not belong in the new moons go. If colours surround you, accept them. Often, when my heart is bound to the pipe in this ceremony, the red blood of life is close beside me and I feel the peace of green beneath me. My mother colour, turquoise blue, fills my energy and protects my sacred pipe.

Each person's spiritual connection is made in the way that is needed at that time during the channupa ceremony. The sacred channupa connects us all and we share our energy, whilst the energy experience remains unique to each one of us. Do not expect. Open your heart and know your connection is safe because it is your own energy vibration merging with the sacred channupa. Your ceremony will naturally give you whatever you need at that time.

Now you are ready for the next stage of the sacred channupa ceremony. Still holding the bowl with your left heart hand, light the pipe with your right hand. Matches are better to use as the more natural the ingredients the better for us, which in turn is better for our Mother, the Earth.

Honour the Creator and the four directions once more in prayer and by pointing the stem of the pipe in each direction. Draw the smoke up through the stem to light the fire in the channupa bowl and in your heart energy.

Smoke the sacred tobacco and blow the message to the Creator, Mother Earth and to grandfather sky. Pray as you smoke. Call upon your ancestors and they will come to help you. There is only one way to pray and that is from a pure heart. The sacred channupa will do the rest. If you are in a group, when you have finished smoking and praying, you can say in the Lakota tongue, 'Mitakuye Oyasin' or 'to all my Relations'. It is not the tongue-language that is important, but the good intention behind the words. Then turn the pipe sun-wise in a full circle and hand it in friendship and with compassion to the person sitting next to you on your left side.

When all the tobacco is smoked, tap out the bowl of the pipe and cover the opening of the bowl with sage. Place this upon the blue cloth that holds your pipe. I utilize the blue cloth for my sacred place or altar as well when I smoke the pipe. I surround the cloth with stones, crystals and other artefacts of special value to me. You can do the same if you wish. Point the stem of the pipe in the direction that speaks to you. Leave the sacred pipe in this position overnight. Then hold the bowl in your left hand and remove the stem with your right hand. Continue to pray as you lay the pipe back inside the blue cloth, still filled with sage until you are ready to do another sacred channupa ceremony.

◄

This sacred channupa can be utilized in many different ways. It is a powerful and beautiful ceremony to share with friends or to smoke alone if you have a specific request. It can also be used before and after a sweat lodge. I often smoke the sacred channupa after a sweat lodge, sharing the tobacco with all of those who have gone through the sacred sweat lodge ceremony with me. I remind them that the pipe must be smoked with peace and trust in their hearts. If you are running a sweat lodge and you are also a pipe carrier, you can do the same. Otherwise, allow the spiritual adviser or medicine person running the sweat lodge to prepare the pipe, say the prayers and light the sacred pipe, sending the prayers high up into the Spirit World, reaching the Creator and connecting with the Energy Source.

It is essential to respect the sacred channupa and honour it as it was intended by sharing it with all those who understand and pray from the heart. The sacred channupa pipe-stone is part of Mother Earth that she shares with the two leggeds. The tobacco that fills the channupa is one of the first plants given to the people of Turtle Island.

The ancient knowledge and healing are carried within the sacred tobacco plant. Mother Earth's pipe-stone and clay blend with the spirit of grandfather sky as we smoke the sacred channupa. The sacred channupa carries our prayers to the Source as the sacred channupa's smoke mirrors our own energy.

Sacred channupa smoke and fire-smoke have long since played a pivotal role in the life of the Native American nations. Smoke signals were used by many nations as they called people to Council or used the smoke signals as warnings of approaching danger. Unlike the smoke signals, the sweat lodge fire-smoke has always been considered sacred. The fire that heats the rocks for the sacred sweat lodge shares a spiritual connection in keeping with the sacred channupa.

5

Rebirth in Mother Earth's Womb

I was born upon the prairie,
Where the wind blew free,
And there was nothing
To break the light of the sun.
I was born where everything
Drew a free breath.

TEN BEARS — COMANCHE

The night fell like a dark blanket from the skies. The daylight was carried away by the night and it slowly called my energy onto the vision plane. I was tired, but my spirit felt restless. My body lay quietly, but my energy was pulled by a strong force onto the vision plane. The Great Grandfather Spirit stood in front of me. His great grandson was by his side. The Great Grandfather said, 'The time has come for you to understand that we are all one. We are connected by the same Energy Source.' The great grandson smiled at his Great Grandfather and the Elder ran his hand through the young boy's shoulder-length black hair. The Great Grandfather Spirit spoke again, 'Close your eyes and rest your spirit, but let your energy blend into ours as we travel back and forward in time.' As his words filled the air, the Great Grandfather Spirit faded away and the little boy went with him.

I closed my eyes as I was asked and my energy joined the blue-grass and I could see the Great Grandfather Spirit and his great grandson standing in front of a small hill. I was in their world, but I was also outside it. I began to understand the parallel nature of energy and time.

The Great Grandfather Spirit looked tired in a way I had seen his energy ebb before. The Elder spoke to the young boy, 'Come my great grandson, let us take a walk to the top of this deep-blue hill. It is called Smoking Hill.' The young boy took the old man's hand and they climbed to the top.

When they reached the summit, they stood together and Great Grandfather Spirit spoke, 'My boy, my young boy, do you know why this hill is called Smoking Hill?' The boy said he did not. Then the Great Grandfather Spirit looked into the distance and was silent for a long time and when he spoke his eyes were welled with sadness. The Great Grandfather Spirit's voice was soft, 'I am old now and I feel my spirit growing restless to be young and free again, but not free as you know freedom, but freedom as it once truly existed in this great land of Turtle Island. It is time you knew about sacred sweat lodges. A sweat lodge was built on this hill for as long as wheat once grew yellow and plentiful among our people on the good lands.'

As the Great Grandfather Spirit's words reached the ears of the young boy, his great grandson saw the Elder's heart grow young and his energy soar with the wind. The Great Grandfather Spirit told the young boy stories through the energy connection about the sacred sweat lodge. The Great Grandfather Spirit smiled at the many visions the sweat lodge ceremonies had given him and what the sweat lodge had taught him when he was a young man.

The Elder shared the time-past with the young boy when the Great Grandfather's own father and grandfather taught him how to build a sacred sweat lodge and how to pray from the heart once inside Mother Earth's womb.

The Great Grandfather Spirit said, 'For many years, our sweat lodges were forbidden and outlawed by Christian missionaries and government officials who did not understand the ceremony or energy connection. Yet, they sensed that there was some hidden power in the sweat lodge and they feared it greatly. Many people have never known what was natural and necessary to us; sacred sweat lodges. The times are changing again, showing us that all time is one. All living things are circular. There is a shift of wind: it comes from the tenacious north, it tells me that the sweat lodge is ready to return, it is needed, it has always been needed.

'The world-society, my boy, has become so strange, so harsh and the earth has been torn asunder like old moccasins that you can't use anymore. So much has changed, not all for the bad, but sadly nearly all, even that which was good in the beginning, has also turned bad. The energy continues to flow, but the connection to the Source is being contaminated. There is much work to be done to reconnect, respect and honour all living things.' The great grandson's eyes filled with tears and he lay his head against his Great Grandfather's arm. The Great Grandfather Spirit said, 'Do not shed tears. We must combine positive energy and build upon our light until healing overtakes the wounding.

'It is a time for peace upon Mother Earth. Time has circled and time has remained, the energy is calling and the two leggeds must respond to the moment of great change. It is in their hands.' Then the Great Grandfather Spirit stretched his arms up towards grandfather sky and chanted as the young boy followed the rhythm with his hands. A strong wind rose up and a few drops of rain fell upon the Great Grandfather Spirit's wise old face.

He smiled up at the blue-grey sky and then turned to the young boy as he winked, 'The connection is within us all. Many will find their own energy pattern as circular time reunites us as one people.' The Great Grandfather Spirit and his great grandson lay down upon the hill and soon their energy was part of it. I could no longer differentiate their energy forms and that of the grass and stones on the sloping hillside. I felt my own energy being drawn towards them, then suddenly, it was pulled back and I woke up.

◄

I had seen sweat lodges built and the sacred ceremonies performed as the Great Grandfather Spirit described them to his great grandson. I was inside the past, but also in the present and yet another part of my energy was in the future. I understood the message that sweat lodges were needed to reunite the two leggeds and bring balance back to Mother Earth. Sweat lodges in themselves symbolize a rebirth inside the earth womb and herald a new beginning. The sacred sweat lodge ceremony links the past, present and future. The sweat lodge's healing heat also unites the two leggeds as one people.

Sacred sweat lodge ceremonies have been performed since ancient times. The Mayans, Eskimos and Druids built these healing and spiritual Mother Earth centres. The sweat lodge's medicinal values were understood from early on and there are numerous stories of how people were healed and purified in the sacred sweat lodge ceremony. Today, society has new diseases and imbalances, but the sweat lodge works in the same way, helping to heal and relieve fevers, rheumatism, asthma and many other human ailments.

Once cleansed and purified in a sweat lodge ceremony, many people experience a strong spiritual connection within the sweat lodge. The sweat lodge often acts as a watery reflection for people and each person faces him – or herself in their own way within this sacred lodge. To confront the deepest part of who you are is not always comfortable at first, but it has wonderful long-term benefits for those who are prepared to open their spirit, heart and eyes.

The spiritual opportunity to look deep within oneself offers insight, new understanding and a clearer pathway and connection to energy. The sweat lodge ceremony will connect those who are ready to the power of the Energy Source, which is ultimately the core of their own being. This knowledge paves the two-legged pathway for the duration of the earth journey.

In the past, the sacred sweat lodge ceremony was an integral part of spiritual preparation and purification for those who wished to offer sweat and a drop of their own blood to Mother Earth during a Sun Dance ceremony. The Sun Dancers would fast and pray for strength as they purified their bodies and spirits in a sweat lodge before they were pierced and danced to the rhythm of the cottonwood tree. After the Sun Dance was over, the dancers would recover and become rejuvenated inside the healing heart-heat of the sweat lodge.

In those days, women were not normally invited into a sweat lodge ceremony or expected to Sun Dance. It was believed that women were already connected to Mother Earth and that their moon cycle cleansed their bodies naturally on a monthly basis. Their moon-time united their blood with Mother Earth's soil as well. Women also gave birth and suffered pain and loss of blood by giving new life to the human race. Native Americans also believe that it was a woman of the Spirit World who gave the people of Turtle Island their first sweat lodge. In accordance with this legend, it was felt that women did not need what was already part of their energy and physical body; the womb.

Life is not so simple for women in the modern world and many are out of balance and need to reconnect with their own energy and Mother Earth's heartbeat. At this time, the sweat lodge ceremony invites all two leggeds, male and female. Both men and women need the sweat lodge ceremony's help to be cleansed, purified and healed. Many people also go to a sweat lodge ceremony in the hope of being spiritually reborn inside the womb of Mother Earth, setting them free to make a fresh start in their lives.

I believe the sweat lodge ceremony also heals Mother Earth; as her children become healthy, so does she, for we are all related. Each energy rebirth resonates universally and affects all living things. My vision had

given me permission to become part of the sweat lodge energy and gather people to purify in spirit, mind and body.

A few weeks after the Great Grandfather Spirit sweat lodge vision, I waited for a medicine man to arrive and lead a sacred sweat lodge. I had taken part in many sweat lodges over the years led by good medicine men, but I had never led one. There were about twenty people who were also waiting for the arrival of the sweat lodge leader. The medicine man did not appear, and the people became uneasy as they were in preparation for the sweat lodge ceremony. The Energies spoke and I knew the moment had arrived for me to perform my first sweat lodge ceremony. That seems a long time ago now, but time is a playful friend.

I would like to share the knowledge of the ancient sweat lodge with you upon the understanding that you will honour this sacred ceremony.

Many people build and run sweat lodges throughout the modern world, but it often saddens me when I discover permission has not been given. Mother Earth is not honoured and the understanding of the energy of this ancient and sacred ceremony is limited. When a sweat lodge is built and the ceremony performed under these conditions, it is doubtful that any healing will be given to the earth or the two leggeds.

Sacred Sweat Lodge Ceremony

I will tell you, my friends, how to build a sweat lodge. Again, I must impress upon you that you can only build and hold a sweat lodge ceremony if you have had a vision that gives you permission. It is true to say, only a few people are called upon to perform a sacred sweat lodge ceremony. So, it is necessary to have your vision confirmed more than once if you wish to perform a sweat lodge ceremony.

You must also be knowledgeable in the practices of sweat lodges. The energy connection is extremely powerful and, like all power, if it is not handled responsibly and with respect it becomes dangerous. The sweat lodge is not a place for people to suffer. It is important to regulate the

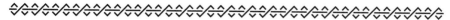

heat so that all two leggeds within the womb of Mother Earth feel safe and protected.

To begin preparing for a sweat lodge, you must search for a sacred site. Preferably, a site that calls you in the night when you are taken upon the vision plane. If you are not granted permission upon the vision plane, you may be out walking and suddenly a sacred energy circle upon the earth will speak to you. Then you know you have found the place to build and hold a sweat lodge ceremony.

A cleansing ceremony must be held in that sacred energy circle before the willows are gathered to build the sweat lodge. The cleansing ceremony means placing tobacco upon Mother Earth and honouring the Creator before smudging the area with sage's cleansing smoke. Only then will the site be prepared for a sweat lodge ceremony.

When the time comes to cut the willow trees, it is important that you speak to the trees, the most ancient of all living things. Remember, the standing people are your friends and some will choose to become part of the sweat lodge ceremony. Ask which one of them wishes to join the sacred sweat lodge and their energy will respond to you. Offer tobacco to the standing people and offer your prayers and gratitude. Also offer tobacco to Mother Earth and honour her for providing us with the standing people who help sustain all living things.

There are many different ways to construct a sweat lodge. I choose to do it as my ancestors built their lodges in the beginning. In this way, I honour my ancestors for the knowledge and wisdom they have passed down to us. I use 28 willow rods, with their permission. Before I begin building, I dig a pit in the centre of the sacred sweat lodge. Later the red-hot lava rocks will be placed in this heart-fire centre. The fire pit will determine the size of the lodge dependent upon the amount of rocks that will heal us with their heat.

From this central heart-fire point, I take a string and measure the distance leading me to the earth-holes for the standing people willows to take root in the ground. I make 28 earth-holes in accordance with the number of willows.

Then the Energies choose the doorway where the people will enter and that will be the first direction I will call upon inside the sacred sweat lodge. This doorway will also be opened briefly after the end of each sacred round of ceremony. There are four ceremonial rounds. Each time the doorway is opened, more grandfather and grandmother rocks are brought in to replenish the heart-fire inside. The opened doorway also allows the spirit of the wind to cool the participants inside the sacred lodge.

Then it is time to walk in a sun-wise direction. I pray as I walk and offer tobacco to each of the 28 willow earth-holes. I finish my prayers when I have completed a full sun-circle and arrive back at my first doorway. I pray to the standing people willows and thank them for agreeing to take part in the ceremony, then I place the willows in the earth-holes. Initially, I take two willows and bend them towards each other until they become one and form an archway over the sacred doorway.

The standing people willows are sealed together as I fasten them with a piece of string that I have included in offerings and prayers. In a sun-wise direction, I begin my circular walk again until all the standing people willows are joined together to create a sacred rounded dome-shaped arbour.

When I unite the standing people willows together as I construct the bones of the sweat lodge in preparation for its skin, I sing happy songs and pray for all of those who will share the sweat lodge ceremony. I also pray for those who cannot attend the ceremony and my prayers include all living things. The positive energy heightens and blends with the energy of the sweat lodge as cheerful songs and compassionate prayers connect with the Energy Source.

My ancestors used buffalo hide to cover their standing people, willow-bone structure. Nowadays, we use a canvas tarp or blankets or both. The heart-intention is the same, to create a soothing, warm earth-womb. This womb, like a mother's, needs to be dark and safe. The blankets must be secured with string and kept in place with the weight of the sitting people, stones. The earth from our mother that is dug out to create a heart-fire is taken outside and utilized to make an altar a few feet away from the

doorway of the sweat lodge. I speak to Mother Earth and thank her for allowing us to utilize her in this way.

A special pit needs to be dug for the fire outside as well. The outside fire should burn with vibrant energy as it heats the rocks. Offer more tobacco and continue to pray. I dig a one-inch straight line from the outside fire to the altar right up to the doorway. This connects them together and represents the umbilical cord of life. It also symbolizes the oneness of all things and emphasizes that we are related.

I place tobacco offerings in coloured ties and secure them on separate sticks around the outside of the sweat lodge as I honour each of the four directions. My tobacco ties hold my prayers. I use the colours red, yellow, black and white because there is no dividing colour and we are all brothers and sisters of the two-legged family.

I also place the same-coloured tobacco ties inside the sweat lodge, uniting the inside of my heart with the outside. Many people place their tobacco ties and other precious objects or artefacts upon the altar. In other sweat lodges, some spiritual advisers or medicine men choose to build their altars inside the lodge. If you are running the sweat lodge, you must decide in accordance with what the Energies have directed.

I use lava rocks as my ancestors have done before me. Choosing the sitting people, rocks, is like choosing the standing people, willows: only those that talk to you and wish to be part of the ceremony can be included in the lodge. Otherwise, the sitting people will explode when heated. Again, understand your brothers and sisters, the sitting people, and give them the love and respect they have always given you.

Offer tobacco and give thanks. The ideal size of the rock should be that of a cantaloupe. If you are not running the sweat lodge ceremony, the spiritual adviser or medicine person will tell you the number of rocks to use. In my own sweat lodge ceremonies, the number of rocks varies in accordance with the needs of the people, Mother Earth and what I feel is needed at that time. Whatever the number, one must begin with seven rocks. The rocks must be revered and carefully set down in a special way one by one into the fire-pit outside the sweat lodge to be heated in preparation before they

become part of the heart-fire inside. As each rock is placed, it must be honoured separately and tobacco offered to the Creator, the four directions, Mother Earth and grandfather sky.

Once the first six rocks are in a circular position with the seventh rock laid in the centre of the fire for the Creator, it is time to bring all the other rocks to join the fire. I place them again in a circular ritual on top of the first seven rocks. It is important to remember to offer tobacco to each rock. Then I surround the rocks with wood and light it. Again, only natural materials should be used. On the inside of the sweat lodge, the bottom of the connecting heart-fire can be covered in sage or flat cedar as it awaits the heat of the rocks.

A special person is chosen to become the fire-keeper of the sacred sweat lodge. The fire-keeper must have a pure energy and a compassionate heart that cares for other people. Native Americans consider it an honour to be selected as a fire-keeper. The fire-keeper makes an energy connection with the fire and the sweat lodge ceremony as he tends the fire. The fire-keeper is also regarded as the protector or guardian of those inside the sweat lodge.

The fire-keeper opens the doorway after ceremonial prayers have been completed, allowing fresh air to cool those who sweat. The fire-keeper works with the fire and rock energies and he often connects with the power of the Energy Source as he keeps vigil outside the sweat lodge door.

There can be extreme heat in the sweat lodge as the prayers progress and people dress accordingly. Normally, people choose to wrap a towel around themselves. Other two leggeds prefer to wear a bathing suit or swimming trunks. The style of dress is up to each individual, but it is important that you remain as comfortable as possible.

The purity of the heart, mind and body must be respected and honoured at all times during the sweat lodge ceremony.

I ask each person to walk around the fire outside in accordance with the sun's direction before they enter the sacred sweat lodge. I request that each person say, 'Mitakye Oyasin' or 'to all my Relations', as they enter the open doorway. They will be asked to sit in an allocated place until a full circle within the sweat lodge is complete.

The fire-keeper fills a large container or bucket with water, then adds a dipper and passes them to me inside the sweat lodge. The dipper is used to pour water onto the rocks when the ceremony begins. The container of water is traditionally brought in after the first seven rocks. I offer the water container to the rocks by touching it lightly upon the hot rocks.

This is a sign of gratitude to the rocks and it also unites the two energies as they work together. I also utilize sacred tobacco, sage, cedar, sweetgrass and osha by sprinkling the sweet-smelling herbs and plants upon the steaming hot rocks.

The osha root has great medicinal properties, like all other sacred herbs. A little piece of osha or sage can be chewed by those inside the sweat lodge if they so wish. Each time the fire-keeper brings in a new rock, I place it inside the heart-fire and cedar-energy is burned upon it.

Cedar is the first herb to be honoured and to honour the rocks because cedar trees often grow out of rock crevices. In this way, the connection of the cedar tree is close to the energy of the rocks and it is felt that their energies belong together. When the sweat lodge ceremony begins, tobacco, sage and sweetgrass are also added to the rocks. The rocks become hotter as the healing within begins. The sweat lodge must remain in perfect darkness with the flap firmly closed as the heat and energy rise during the sacred ceremony.

The sweat lodge has the four elements of fire, water, air and earth. Once the fire-keeper has brought in the first seven rocks followed by the water, I lay the sacred herbs upon each rock, praying all the while, 'Grandfather, grandmother rocks, have pity upon us and hear our prayers.' A potent and beautiful scent fills the air from the herb-coated burning rocks. An overwhelming feeling of friendship and compassion frequently fills the sweat lodge, especially when those sharing the sweat are pure hearted and united in their love for Mother Earth and all living things.

If the first direction is south, then I call upon the southern energies in the first doorway as I offer the first cup of water to the sitting people, the rocks. The first doorway refers to the first direction. If it is south, then the second doorway will be west, then north and east.

In the sweat lodge, the south represents the wonder of life. Whilst the water is sizzling upon the rocks, I advise the two leggeds that this is a good time to ask their relatives and ancestors to help them receive the cleansing and purification this ceremony can provide. The steam and fire-smoke carry the prayers to the Creator. It is a good moment to thank Mother Earth for allowing us into her womb for a sacred ceremony.

A drum can be played by the lodge leader or an eagle bone whistle gently blown to call in the Energies. I often use an eagle bone whistle, calling upon the energy of the eagle as I play the whistle. A rattle can also be utilized to call the Energies. The water is a life giver and I thank the Creator for the water as I pour it on the rocks. If the two leggeds within the sweat lodge request greater heat, I pour a little extra water upon the sitting people.

During the sweat lodge ceremonies I am careful to maintain a gentle heat in the first doorway. I believe this offers peoples' bodies the chance to adapt to the increasing heat that will follow as the doorways progress.

We must preserve the air and try to clean what has been contaminated. Like those in the sweat lodge, the air that we breathe needs to be cleansed and purified. If we do this, our children and their children's children can enjoy the good, clean air that the Great Spirit gave to us in the beginning.

Many people become aware of their breathing and the beat of their own heart during the first doorway as the body begins to sweat and impurities are washed out. The spirit is also cleansed and purified with prayers. The earth itself connects with those who offer thanks in the sweat lodge as her own rhythm is felt beneath each body, literally and spiritually joining the two leggeds with Mother Earth.

It is the time to unite and show gratitude for the earth we walk and sit upon and to remember each and everyone around you with compassionate feelings and prayers.

The first doorway is relatively short, depending upon the way it is performed. In the sweat lodge ceremonies I lead, the first doorway lasts for approximately 20 minutes. This is the shortest doorway and after it is finished, the door is opened, allowing cool, refreshing air to blow gently upon all those who sweat.

During this period many people like to ask questions and some medicine people are happy to answer, others feel that it interferes with the Energies. For the most part, I encourage people to talk and voice any fears they might have.

Many two leggeds will speak of visions or fear initially, followed by elation after the experience of their first sweat lodge. Whatever needs to be said, I welcome it, for we are all related and each one of us has questions and others can learn from the question as well as the answer.

The second doorway, in accordance with the sun-wise position, will be the west as we started in the south. The third door will represent the north and the fourth door will honour the east.

The fire-keeper brings in the next round of rocks for the second door and I give them thanks and honour the sitting people with sacred herbs in the same way as the first seven rocks. The second round is the healing round and if any person feels spiritually, mentally or physically sick, they can either ask for special prayers from everyone to heal them, or they can pray silently.

By this time, I will have already explained that this is a healing round and many people will ask for guidance. I say to them, 'Whatever you feel, your pain or suffering, it is also felt by Mother Earth. Look at the origin of your discomfort and pain. Trace your steps back and ask the Creator and the Energies to help heal the origin of the pain. We will all pray for you.

'When we pray for you, we are also praying for ourselves because our energy is interconnected. The power of the mind to heal is strong, but the heart is stronger and the spirit stronger still. Look to grandfather sky: when you see those silver raindrops, those are tears for you and for all those who endure sickness. Mother Earth will help you become one with yourself again and at one with all that breathes upon her back. Healing comes from within your own energy and heart. May this sweat lodge ceremony help you upon the pathway of healing and connection to the Energy Source.'

I often offer people a small piece of osha root or sage to chew in the second, healing round because of its medicinal and soothing properties. The second round is hotter as the heat pushes imbalances out of the body. The second doorway is often called the Balancing of Spirit, Mind and Body as it helps all three to balance as a harmonious energy.

It is time for the third round to begin. Again, it is essential to care for each two legged within the sacred sweat lodge, ensuring that each person feels comfortable and prepared for the increased heat of the third door. The fire-keeper brings in more red-hot rocks for the third doorway.

The third doorway invites people to pray out loud if they wish, one at a time, or to pray silently if they prefer. I ask each person to say, 'To all my relations' when they have completed their prayer, letting the person to the immediate left know that they have finished and the next person may begin.

The energies of the north are called upon in this third doorway. Knowledge and wisdom are called to help overcome ignorance, greed and hatred. This door also represents the red peace channupa. It symbolizes friendship and trust.

After the third doorway, I offer a drink of water to those participating in the sweat lodge ceremony. I remember one man remarking, 'Water never tasted so good'. We can take so much for granted, disrespect and apathy can set in through lack of awareness and appreciation.

When you are only allowed one mouthful of water in the parching heat, you savour it and feel grateful. Prayers of thanks are given naturally. I advise people to take only one mouthful of water because if you drink too much water in the sweat lodge it can interfere with the cleansing process. The toxins in the body must be sweated out. After the sweat lodge ceremony is completed, you can drink as much water as you wish.

The fourth and last door is the east door. All the energies and ancestors come together in the fourth door to help heal us and Mother Earth. Many people say they experience spiritual growth during the last doorway. Sacred songs and prayers are offered, led by the spiritual adviser or medicine man.

The sweat group join together as one voice to thank the Creator and the Energies for a good sweat and for all the healing they have been given. Allow the rocks to cool and remain seated until you feel it is time for you to leave. As each person passes out through the doorway, I ask them to say, 'Mitakye Oyasin' or 'We are all Related.'

If I continue to run the same sweat lodge, then it is left with its willows exposed to nature as they were before. The tarp or blankets are removed and kept safe and dry for the next sacred sweat lodge ceremony. I surround the sweat lodge with tobacco before I leave it in preparation for the next sweat lodge ceremony.

If I intend to use the sweat lodge only once, then I honour the sweat lodge and willows by burning the lodge. This allows the sweat lodge and standing people to go home and return to the Energy Source.

I believe a two legged's first sweat ceremony cleanses and purifies the body as well as reconnecting each human being to Mother Earth. If a person continues to participate in sacred sweat lodge ceremonies, then the hidden or hurt parts within can be healed as they slowly come to the surface. This can be a difficult process at first, as many people do not wish to face the wounds inside, but over time, the pain lessens as knowledge and wisdom deepen. Some people are not even aware that they have been wrestling with inner conflicts for many years until they participate in a sweat lodge ceremony. Yet, like all wounds, if they are neglected they can fester and spread to other areas. Once the inner turmoil is recognized and brought to the surface, it is more difficult to push it back down again and the only real choice is to deal with it.

When the hurt and source of pain are understood and accepted, then healing and recovery can begin. The sacred sweat lodge ceremony will continue to help once the inner healing is done because it is then that the powerful Energy Source connection commences.

During the life of the Old Ways, the sweat lodges' healing power and connection to the Energy Source was understood. Many warriors and other two leggeds utilized the sweat lodge to prepare for a vision quest.

The sweat lodge ceremony opened the doorway to the Energy that allowed them to walk upon the vision plane. The two leggeds called upon the Creator, the Energies and their ancestors to keep them safe as they sought a vision. It was often within the sacred sweat lodge that they received the knowledge they needed before they began their spiritual journey upon the vision quest. Those who sweated also received other valuable information that helped them as they abstained from food and drink. The seekers prepared themselves by spending four days and nights seeking a vision with a medicine person keeping a discreet distance to make sure they were safe. The Great Grandfather Spirit allowed me to vision alongside the energy-memory of his own first vision quest.

6

◄

Time Within Time of the Vision Quests

The visions that come upon a Vision Quest
Have a sacred power all of their own.
WA-NA-NEE-CHE

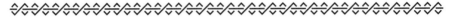

The night was heavy with the scent of perfumed blossoms. Nature was tantalizing and I felt a magnetic energy pulling me through sweet-smelling, soft white planes. I could hear the Great Grandfather Spirit chanting as I journeyed into the vision world. The Great Grandfather sang and danced in a sun-wise circle. His great grandson followed the Elder's steps before their dance-paths criss-crossed as the rhythm increased. Their energy became one as they swirled into blue and red clouds of movement. The colours flowed in and out, creating a lightning rainbow of energy-light. I heard a child laugh before the colours were sucked back into the human form of the Great Grandfather Spirit and his great grandson.

The Great Grandfather Spirit and the young boy stood hand in hand in front of me. My eyes closed and I could see a time when vision quests rose and met the spirit like the morning sun amongst the Native American people. I recognized this as a sign to walk upon the pathway that would lead me to become as one with the true meaning of vision quests.

The Great Grandfather Spirit and his great grandson darkened and the light slowly faded all around. A single bright light shone where the Great Grandfather and the young boy had stood and this sunny light spread until I could see many people camped beside a deep brown river. I looked closely towards the origin of the brilliant yellow light and I could see a boy who was no more than eleven summers.

The young boy looked like the great grandson. An old man sat speaking to the young boy in a tipi marked with many black and white horse paintings. I did not realize who they were at first, but as the Elder spoke, I recognized his voice; the tongue belonged to the Great Grandfather Spirit, but simultaneously I understood that the young boy was also the Great Grandfather Spirit. At the same time, the Great Grandfather Spirit remained within the form of the Elder I had come to know so well in my many visions. The multiplicity of time and power of the energy connection resonated within me as the Great Grandfather Spirit spoke of his first vision quest.

The Great Grandfather told the young boy that vision quests were as vital to the Native American people as sweat lodges and all other sacred

ceremonies. The Great Grandfather Spirit said, 'When my time had come to be a man, I asked the Creator for a vision. I needed to know my life's pathway so that I could place my feet in the direction intended for my earthwalk. I was little more than a child, just one moon older than you, but our lands had already been disturbed and the omens spoke of the dark locust days that lay ahead.

'Our medicine man, Yellow Bird, found me sitting by a brook throwing stones into the water. Yellow Bird sat down beside me, "So, you are ready to become a man," he said. I had not told him, but like many powerful medicine men, words are not always necessary.

'I replied, "Yes, I am, but I seek a vision so that the Creator can tell me which pathway to follow that will lead me to the truth." The medicine man laid one hand on my left shoulder, "Son, I will have you in my family for one year to prepare you for your vision quest. You will have to eat special foods and herbs, you must observe this strict diet for one year. You will have to run every day until you can keep pace with a horse. Learn to be skilled with a bow and arrow because soon you will understand that the energy connection will give you the concentration you need. There are other things you must do to prepare physically for a vision quest, but most of all you must meditate and pray every day and every night for the vision you want the Creator to show you. Offer tobacco, burn sage and give thanks. After one year, if you do all I say, you will be ready to go on a vision quest." '

The Great Grandfather Spirit waited for a moment and looked into the eyes of his young great grandson who listened without stirring or asking a question. The Great Grandfather Spirit continued, 'I knew this would be a year to test as well as to prepare me for a vision quest. I had to prove I had a strong spirit, heart and body. I needed to develop skills that my life would depend upon as a man and a warrior. Most of all, I needed to let the medicine man and elders know that I was pure-hearted in my intentions and mature enough to take whatever the Creator would show me, good or bad.

'There are stories, you know, of men who went on vision quests and afterwards, they no longer spoke or laughed. People say it was because they

were not prepared for the quest and not ready to see their life drawn out before them like a detailed sand-picture.

'There were still others who were too young or too arrogant and did not take the advice of the medicine man who helped them and interpreted the language of their visions. Everyone knows that only those who are connected to the Energy Source can understand the language of visions.' The Great Grandfather Spirit rested and let the many moons that had passed drift away until he was a boy of eleven summers again.

When his energy returned to his great grandson, he was smiling to himself, 'Ah, did I work for that year I spent with Yellow Bird and his family. I had to rise before the sun and pray, pray, pray. I prayed so hard all day and all night. I ate the foods and herbs that Yellow Bird's wife, Bear Claw Woman, prepared for me. I chased antelopes until I could catch up and become part of the four-legged energy. Then I went to my horse, Storm Runner, and I told him what was expected of me. I asked him if he would teach me to run as fast as he could, like the wind, without effort. Storm Runner's energy agreed to help me and every day we ran together until I understood every muscle and movement in his strong, black body.

'Storm Runner was a good teacher, he was kind and patient, as the four leggeds often are with the two leggeds. Storm Runner knew I was not as powerful as he was, but he taught me many secrets and in the end, I ran neck to neck with him. Storm Runner was young, like me, but he had already learned much. His heart was full of spirit and it was within his breed to give until their last drop of blood was spent.

'I never loved a horse as much as Storm Runner. The energy between us was made before us and has continued after our earth life finished. Storm Runner came to take me upon his back when my time had come to ride into the Spirit World many long years afterwards. Time folding into time, my young boy. I was telling you about vision quests and we cannot confuse time and energy until they are fully understood. It is time to share the knowledge of my first vision quest.

'For many, one vision quest is enough and for some, it is one too many. After twelve months was over I had grown tall and as strong as a young elk.

Yellow Bird told me that I had followed and passed all the rites for a vision quest. Yellow Bird looked at me a long time before he said I was ready to join him in a sacred sweat lodge ceremony. Yellow Bird said, "After the purification of the sweat lodge, I will take you to the top of Buffalo Hill. Then you will be alone for four days and nights. You will not eat or drink anything during this period. You may take a blanket and a medicine bag with you. I will give you a sacred channupa that I have made myself for the purpose of your vision quest.

' "You will smoke the channupa on Buffalo Hill and keep it with you as long as your legs walk upon this earth. This is all you can take. When you come down, you will be a man and you, my son, will have seen things that no-one else will see in the same way, although many may be given similar knowledge. This is the power of the Energy Source."

'I talked to Storm Runner before I left and asked him to send his strong spirit to help me if I needed it, for this was going to be a time of great personal battle for four days and nights. Storm Runner's energy rushed towards me and I felt safe. I said goodbye to my family and my mother, who I had not been in contact with for one year. My mother broke down and wept when I collected my blanket from her. My father said, "Go, you are a boy now, but you will return as a man."

'Yellow Bird and I climbed in silence to the top of Buffalo Hill. I sat on my blanket, holding the channupa he had made for me. Yellow Bird looked all around the hill and then he said, "I offer tobacco to the Creator, the four directions, Mother Earth and grandfather sky, to keep this young boy safe during his vision quest." Yellow Bird placed the tobacco sun-wise honouring the four directions around where I sat. Then, without another word, he left me. It was only when I was a grown man that I learned Yellow Bird remained on Buffalo Hill, secretly guarding me from a distance during my vision quest.

'For the first two nights I sang many sacred songs and continued to pray for a vision, never moving from the sacred circle, but nothing came. By the third night, I was so tired and hungry that my head began to throb. I felt my body tremble as I fell forward. I fought the need to sleep with angry fists. Then Storm Runner appeared before me. I thought I had failed and that

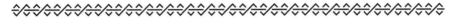

they had sent him to bring me home. I shouted, "Go away, I must have a vision. I will not leave this hill until my quest is finished."

'Storm Runner tossed his black mane and reared onto his hind legs before pouring water on top of my head from his mouth. "Stop, I cannot drink!" I shouted, but the water splashed harder, and when I looked up, Storm Runner had gone and the skies had opened to spill down upon Buffalo Hill and me. Thunder roared and streaks of silver-white lightning lit up the hill. My body began to shake with cold and something called fear crept up behind me and held me tightly by the throat.

'I was afraid I would shed tears, remember I was very young. Suddenly a strong wind rushed across the hill and knocked the fear right out of me. I shouted at the wind, "I am not afraid of you! The Creator will protect me. No matter what you do, I will not leave here until my vision quest is over." The wind turned south, then changed in fury back towards the east where I sat. It almost blew me out of the sacred circle, but I clung to the ground like a cornered animal. A blinding, violet-red light filled the sky and sent a bolt of burning orange hurtling towards me. I covered my eyes, believing I would be killed, but when I dared to look again, the storm had left.

'The hill was as quiet as a grave, I almost wished the storm would return. I felt a change in the earth, the quietness crept into my ears and I tried to prepare myself for the vision I knew would surely come.

'A young woman stood before me wearing a white buckskin dress that fell to her bare feet. She spoke, "There is nothing to tell you. Your life will not be as those who came before you.

' "The day of your people is almost over. You will fight with many other young braves trying to reverse the change of the moon, but nothing will come of it, because in the end you will be driven like four leggeds and penned in, reliant on your enemy and forced to live on the bad lands. Even your own people will turn like the magpie and steal from each other in the night. This is why I say there is nothing to tell you. This is the beginning of your end and that of your people." The woman paused and closed her eyes. As she opened her eyes she spoke again, "Be patient, wait, wait for moon

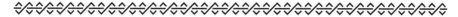

after moon to give way to sun after sun. It is only then that the original energy will be as one again. The sacred tree will call upon all people and the sacred hoop will be mended." The storm rose up with greater force than before and knocked me out of the sacred circle.

'I awoke many days later lying on my father's bed. Yellow Bird had carried me down from the hill on the fifth day. I burned with a sweating fever for many days and nights. During that time, I was not with the two-legged world, but I was told that Yellow Bird gave me strong medicine herbs. When I finally returned to the living place I saw Yellow Bird's face. Yellow Bird looked aged through lack of sleep. Yellow Bird knew that I would recover and said, "You have come back to us, now I will go and rest." After that fever-world which followed my vision quest, many people asked me, "What did you see? Where did you go?" I just shook my head and refused to speak. I was afraid to tell them.

'Yellow Bird returned after some days had passed and waited for me to speak. I sat mute-still until finally Yellow Bird broke the silence, "Is it so terrible that you cannot speak of it? You know it is the face of visions and maybe you need help to understand it."

'I asked Yellow Bird to walk a short distance with me, near the river so that no-one else could hear what I had to say. We sat beside the river and I looked into its brown water pools trying to find courage for what I was about to tell him. Finally, my tongue broke loose and spoke without pausing, "A woman came dressed in white buckskin, she said there was nothing to tell me because our way of life was at an end. She said we would be imprisoned and even turn against each other. Then, she said, after many, many moons, more than anyone can count, had passed, we would return as one people and the sacred hoop would be mended."

'Yellow Bird looked towards a grove of cottonwood trees before speaking, "So it is coming what many great elders and medicine men and women have already seen. I smelt it in the air, the bad changes are crawling towards us. You are a man now and you are also a warrior. If a warrior is to die in battle, then that is a good death, but to be stripped of your honour and turn against your own people, no man can bear this humiliation. Pray

you die fighting the good fight to keep the freedom we have always known."
We never spoke of my vision again.

'It was not for me to go to the Spirit World at that time, although I fought
many, many battles. I lived while others returned to their spiritual home.
Sometimes, I felt I had lived too long and in the end, I began to look like an
ancient, knotted oak tree. The woman in white buckskin never returned to
me in visions, but her words came to life and then life was taken. As more
life was taken and the atrocities worsened with each passing day, there were
times when I could feel the strange presence of the hopeful future the spiritual woman had foretold.

'I tried to share the vision knowledge with the other warriors. I said,
"Many of our ways are destroyed and we look like a broken bough hanging
upon a tree, but remember, everything broken will be mended in the circular healer of time. The Creator and the Energies have not deserted us. This
is a time within a time and yet there will be a greater time, when we are all
one people, even more than we were before the bad troubles started." '

The Great Grandfather Spirit's voice tailed off until I could not hear
what he was saying. A chant replaced the Great Grandfather's words and a
drumbeat resounded in the village that followed the river-song. Darkness
engulfed the tipis until there was just one tiny, yellow light left. As I looked
at this spark of yellow, I woke up. The air was heavy with black clouds and
before long it was raining. As the rain fell, I could see the image of a black
horse in the dark clouds.

The concepts of time and human life as we know it circled within my
own energy. I was drawn to ancient memories and stories I had heard from
the past when many people journeyed to the vision plane naturally and
therefore did not need to seek a vision quest. Some nations describe it as
crying for a vision. Similar to the sweat lodge, in the old days, many Native
American nations did not believe it was necessary for women to go upon
vision quests as they were already connected to the Source. This belief was
further endorsed by the fact that it was usually the spirit of a woman who
came and gave men the wisdom they sought whilst on a vision quest.

Night on the Hill Ceremony

Today, with the turning tide and the search for spiritual meaning, many people, male and female, wish to go on a vision quest. They are eager to find themselves, but first they must understand what it is they seek. A vision quest still holds the same principles, but has been adapted to fit our earth-time as we understand it. You no longer have to run as fast as a horse, but you do have to be physically fit and well.

A healthy diet is always required and prayers from the heart are vital for the vision quest journey. It still takes about one year to prepare for a vision quest and it must never be undertaken alone. A pure-hearted, renowned spiritual adviser or medicine man or woman must be sought. When you feel satisfied that you have found the right person for you and he or she agrees to prepare and take you through a vision quest, then it is right for you to go. You must feel an energy connection between the spiritual adviser or medicine person with your own energy. He or she will tell you what you need and you must follow the instructions throughout the quest for your own safety and well being.

People often have high expectations from vision quests and look for a life-changing experience. In the past, such visions happened more frequently as people were more connected to the Energy Source. Nowadays, there is more internal work to be done with each person before they are ready to embrace some of the visions they seek.

The Oglala Sioux called upon the energy of tobacco, sage and sweet-grass when they cried for a vision. The Oglala warrior would go to an elder or medicine man and offer tobacco to honour the gift of the elder or medicine man. The tobacco was also given in gratitude and as a sign of respect. The vision seeker and medicine man would speak about the heart-energy of the vision and why it was required. If the medicine man agreed that a vision quest would help the warrior, then the medicine man would pray and offer tobacco before accompanying the person who underwent the vision quest.

A four-day fast would begin in seclusion within a tobacco circle, often inside a prayer lodge. The medicine man would sit close by offering prayers and sacred songs for the person within the lodge. Each day the medicine man would smudge outside the prayer lodge with sacred sage to cleanse and purify and rid the area of any negative energy.

A willow branch was often cut to the height of the man seeking the vision. The willow pole was used as a ceremonial object to symbolize the two legged. The willow was placed centrally and surrounded by tobacco, honouring the Creator and four directions at the beginning of the vision quest ceremony. Sage was also added to the tobacco circle, giving added protection to the vision seeker. More sage was placed within the medicine circle, so that the vision seeker could feel the energy of the sage combined with Mother Earth's energy forces. The Oglala Sioux vision seeker sat within the sacred vision circle for four days and four nights without moving, eating, drinking or sleeping.

Tobacco ties and an eagle's feather were often tied upon the willow pole to draw the winged one's energy. The Oglala Sioux called upon the energy of sweetgrass to appease the apparitions of frightening visions and used the sage to protect their own spirit energy. The vision seeker sang sacred songs and chanted for the vision he felt he needed to guide him upon his pathway. Prayers were offered from the heart and the medicine man observed the two-legged seeker until he was satisfied that the person had completed his quest.

The medicine man would help the vision seeker to rejoin the physical world after four days and nights. The medicine man would also help to interpret the meaning and symbolism of the visions the seekers could not understand.

In the modern world, many people ask for a four-day vision quest, but I believe that most two leggeds are not physically or spiritually prepared for such a long quest these days. A group of people I had spent many months working with felt they were ready for a vision quest. After seeking my own guidance and getting permission from the Energies, I agreed to help four people spend one night on the hill.

◂

A dark grey-green hill was chosen to spend a vision quest night upon as this hill had spoken to many people in the group. I offered tobacco to the Creator, the Energies, the four directions and then to the hill itself for granting us permission to honour it. I burned sacred sage and smudged along the pathway where we walked. Once each person had chosen where they wished to sit, I smudged the area and the two leggeds with sage and cedar.

The night was warm, but it was necessary for all four people to wrap a blanket around themselves. They had prayed and offered tobacco to the Creator and Energies for two days prior to the vision quest upon the hill. Two people had chosen to fast for 48 hours prior to the quest.

I knew that the two people who had chosen to fast were physically fit and they were also used to long meditations. The other two people fasted for 24 hours before the night of their vision quest. Although I do not feel it is necessarily so important to abstain from food, it is essential that spiritual preparation, prayers and tobacco offerings are made before going on a vision quest.

I sang sacred songs and chanted as the four vision seekers sat upon the hill as nightfall began to gently turn the hill from green to black. Just before the night settled in, I performed a fire ceremony. I spoke to the rocks and asked their permission to aid the journey of the two leggeds upon the hill. I did the same with the wood as I offered tobacco and prayer to give thanks. A golden-orange glow lit one side of the hill. The group had their backs to the fire and their eyes closed. The fire was close enough to offer some warmth, but not too close, otherwise the fire could distract the sitting two leggeds. I sat beside the fire and prayed for those upon their vision quest. I asked the Creator to grant them the help and guidance they sought. The hill was as quiet as those who sat upon her green back. The only sound I could hear was the occasional hiss and whistle when water released from the wood met the heat or a splinter cracked into the night air. As I prayed, I watched the vision seekers throughout the night.

Dawn broke early with rays of shy yellow dipping colour onto the hill. The four vision seekers remained seated and within their own worlds. I fed some wood to the fire and began to prepare a hot breakfast for those who had not eaten for some time. The first person to join me to eat was Toosa. I looked at the rising sun and was able to gauge the time as 7am.

When Toosa and I spoke in the past, she often expressed a fervent wish that a particular question might be answered by going upon a vision quest. Toosa said that this question had plagued her since childhood and she felt if she could find the answer, the knowledge would release her. Toosa did not give any more details. I believed this woman would find her way without a vision quest as she frequently went to the vision plane where the Energies taught her. Toosa was impatient as she felt her request was urgent and she was keen to get onto her true pathway. Before the night on the hill, Toosa gave a wry smile, 'The Energies come as they will, but just when I am asleep, I cannot summon them. I would like to go and talk to them whilst awake, so that we can meet with my eyes open.' I asked her, 'Are your eyes not open in the vision world?' She laughed and agreed that they were, but her heart was set on a vision quest and so she became one of the vision seekers who sat upon the hill.

Toosa drank some water and ate a little bread, but refused the hot food. She seemed preoccupied and I waited for her to speak. Finally, she said, 'Nothing much happened for the first three or four hours, then I saw a big, hazy blue mountain.

'There was a golden blaze near the top of the mountain, then the image faded. After that another mountain, the same velvet blue colour, appeared quickly with gold dazzling at the top. As I sat there on my hill, one blue mountain after another came before me, always with the same gold near or on the top. I became exhausted watching the mountains and all the while I kept thinking, "What does this mean? Why are all these mountains appearing with a golden light at the top?" I felt light-headed, but knew I could not, would not move. Finally, after I do not know how long, the mountains faded away and I was out of my body, or at least my spirit was away from my physical being. I stood at the foot of a large hill. Although in the vision-state, I could not see the top of the hill, and yet at the same time I was at the top of the hill. There was one feather stuck in the top of the hill. The bottom half of the feather was deep brown and the top was a piercing turquoise blue. There was a black circle outlined and etched in the middle of the feather. Then it was morning and I guess my quest was over, although I have no idea what any of it means.'

Toosa poured some hot tea and sat upon the ground, staring pensively into the comfort of the fire, 'I feel more mystified than ever. I certainly was not given a clear answer.' She looked at me as she finished speaking, waiting for an explanation. As humans, we complicate things to the point where we do not understand colour, symbolism or sacred objects any more. Toosa waited for me to say something, but I remained silent and then she laughed, 'I was so impatient for this vision. Maybe it is not time for me to know or understand the answer to my question yet. I would like to wait and see if I can figure it out. This is for me to unfold and interpret.' I knew that in time Toosa would understand her own vision and learn to speak its language.

Toosa and I met again some months later. She told me that she understood her vision because other visions followed that clarified the night on the hill's vision. Toosa said, 'The mountains symbolized the hurdles I must cross in my life. They are the challenges that I will have to overcome and they are all within myself. Self-doubt and fear are my personal mountains that I must climb, or maybe I can even go around the odd one. The hill was my arrival and I did not even have to climb it. My strength and determination led me to the hill and my energy became powerful. The feather, well, I believe the feather's colours are significant as the feather is myself. The earth brown at the bottom is my connection to the earth itself. The turquoise blue at the top is the healing I have done within and the black circle is the continuation of all life.' I asked, 'Has that answered the question that you needed to be resolved?' Toosa shook her head, 'It has answered much more than that, but in a broader sense. I have the confidence to pursue my true pathway now. I will not give up at the first obstacle as I have already passed over so many visionary mountains.' Toosa had received what she sought on the vision quest.

The other two leggeds who spent a night upon the hill seeking a vision did not go into a vision state in the same way Toosa journeyed. It is important to remember that each one will receive what they need at that time, dependent upon their own state of being. One man said to me, 'I have reached a deeper spiritual level and I feel I touched the heart of the hill.'

Another woman had similar feelings to the man, 'I felt closer to myself than I have ever felt before; alone and yet not alone.' The last person said, 'I wanted to do this ceremony to have a vision, but I am happy that I did not go onto the vision plane. I spent the night reviewing my life and I am going to make some changes. I have made serious realizations and I know it will not be easy, but I have to start again, and that means letting go of what is not working.' The hill energy and solitude had helped each person with the areas where they sought guidance.

We prayed in a circle on top of the hill as we offered thanks and tobacco for keeping us safe throughout the night of the quest. As we climbed down the hill I told them a humorous story the elders had told me about a young, arrogant man who desperately wanted to go upon a vision quest.

This young man was convinced he would be chosen by the Energies and given a wondrous vision. Finally, one of the medicine men thought it was time for this young man to learn a lesson. The medicine man began to help him prepare for a vision quest. The night arrived for the young man to go and climb the sacred vision butte.

The young man sat impatiently on the top of the butte whilst the wind blew a merry tune. By the fourth night, the young man had become angry because he had not received the vision he sought.

Then a small, red ant climbed up his leg and spoke to him, 'I have come to talk to you.' The young man brushed the ant off his leg with agitation, 'I do not want to talk to you, a stupid, little crawling creature. I am waiting for a beautiful woman or an eagle, or a white buffalo to come and give me a vision. I do not have time to waste with you.'

The tiny ant's body was covered in dust from the fall and he felt dizzy. Yet the ant was determined and started the long climb back up the man's leg again. Finally, when the ant arrived, gasping for breath, he spoke again,

'Please, listen to me, I have something important to tell you.'

The young man's anger erupted and he jumped up, almost breaking the sacred circle. 'Get off my leg! I told you I am waiting for a vision. Do not bother me again or I will crush you with my little finger.' The ant quivered with fear and began to crawl away, but turned back one last time, 'So, you do not want to hear what I have to tell you?' The young man yelled 'NO!' so loudly that he blew the red ant way up into the skies. The young man sat down again in a worse temper than ever and waited all through the night for a vision to come, but nothing came. On the fifth day, he stomped down the mountain in a vile mood and met the medicine man at the bottom.

The medicine man was doubled in two with helpless laughter. 'Why are you laughing?' the young man shouted at the medicine man. The medicine man laughed even more until he was holding his sides and almost rolling on the ground. The young man shouted at the top of his voice, 'Why are you laughing at me?' The medicine man finally managed to stop laughing, although his face was still beaming with humour. 'You were too good to speak to the red ant, heh? Pity, because it was the Creator who came as a little red ant to bring the great vision you so desperately sought.' The young man was speechless, but it took many more harsh lessons before he finally understood that every living thing is part of the Energy Source which can take many forms.

Time within time, parallel life forces come together when the energy balance is directly connected to the Source. Past, present and future co-exist as a natural law within the energy life of visions. Many people seek a vision quest, specifically to experience the totality of being one with all living things without the constraints of time or physical body weight. Yet, many two leggeds cannot achieve this vision state because they are blocked by anxiety and pre-conceived expectations. Vision quests can enable people to get in touch with their own energy and higher state of being, provided they have prepared themselves through prayer, good thoughts and actions. Many people do not need a vision quest as they can remember their night visions that reveal greater understanding and knowledge of the Old Ways and the Energy Source.

7

◄

Dreams and Vision Journeys

Sometimes dreams are wiser than waking.

But if the vision was true and mighty,
It is true and mighty yet.
BLACK ELK (1863—1950), OGLALA SIOUX

The night sky hung heavy with the sparkling weight of a million stars. I felt the energy vibrations of universal life. Time stood still and at the same second I felt it race across the planets. It circled around me and arrived at the point it started without any noticeable movement. I smiled at the many mysteries grandfather sky shielded. I lay upon my bed and soon the vision world encircled my earth life and all became one as I met the familiar face of the Great Grandfather Spirit. His great grandson was by the Elder's side as before.

By now, I knew I would see through the eyes of the young boy and, simultaneously, through the eyes of the wise, ancient man. My own spirit remained still and yet moved with their combined energy. The Great Grandfather Spirit did not beckon me, but he closed his eyes and our world became one.

I heard the words of Great Grandfather Spirit as he spoke to the young boy, 'In the distant past, a long time ago, yet, as close as yesterday, the two leggeds understood visions and relied upon them to give messages from the Spirit World. When the Old Ways were neglected and thrown to one side, mayhem and spiritual desecration choked the gateway to the Energy Source.' The Great Grandfather Spirit's voice dropped to a whisper and then he fell silent.

I could see the young boy sitting beside his Great Grandfather waiting for the Elder to speak again, 'Many people stopped feeling altogether. This was the time of world energy disturbance. Those who did not understand came from far away and interfered with the natural flow of life and spiritual connection.

'The people of Turtle Island were forced to live in square houses that went against the circular energy of life. Many two leggeds erected tipis at the back of the box houses. They wanted to feel Mother Earth beneath their bodies.

'So it went for many, many moons, and the energy connection became jagged like broken glass within the hearts of the people; anger and despair replaced prayer and hope. As the moons changed, so did the land and free life that had always guided the two leggeds to the Creator. Many opted for the new ways of the oppressor as they became ever more disconnected from their own Source. It was a hard time, because the nations' energies were divided

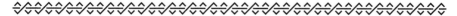

and they were not at one with themselves. Some people held onto the Old Ways and passed the knowledge down the family energy-line and so it was carried from generation to generation. Those people were guided through visions. In their visions they foresaw the circular return of the Old Ways.

'The time we walk during this moon-phase, is a time about to turn back upon itself. The two leggeds are holding out their hands searching in the dark for the connection to the Energy Source.

'Many spirits and Energies reach out to help them and their help is felt by the people.' The Great Grandfather Spirit and his great grandson looked at me. I was about to speak when I woke up with a start, with the unspoken words still formed on my tongue. The vision had ended, but the connection to the vision energy pulsated with life.

Later I would speak to many people about the vision world and how it can be utilized as a key to lead them to the Energy Source. Many two leggeds expressed confusion and said they did not know if their night-time was spent dreaming or if they embarked upon a vision journey.

The easiest way to understand the difference between a dream and a vision is to understand the purpose of both. The transforming energy of visions is a direct link to the Energy Source. Visions can give great knowledge and wisdom once you understand its energy language.

Dreams are also guides, but they work on a human, psychological level, allowing people to work out subconscious or conscious problems and fears. Those dreams that many people call nightmares, are really your warriors, strong enough to fight what you cannot face during your waking hours. Your subconscious is exposed during dreaming hours and many deep-rooted and difficult personal issues are resolved. Problems that need to be solved will turn into recurring dreams until you are able to deal with them. Negative and resentful feelings that gnaw at your insides, struggling to be released, can be set free in dreams. Otherwise, those negative forces can remain stuck, and like all unhealed wounds, they eventually turn septic. Dreams open the gateway to healing.

Once you begin to understand the message in your dreams, you will start to come to terms with psychological problems and your pathway will clear.

After you have been in the dream-state, and you have looked at the problem and dealt with it, even partially, you will feel better than you have felt for a long time.

You will be amazed at how quickly your life begins to improve as your cleared pathway allows you to walk where your energy was always destined to go. The psychological debris will clear as long as you work with the dream and do not deny its teaching methods. The dreams, once understood and resolved, will give way to the spiritual world of visions.

In contrast to dreams, visions are extraordinarily vivid. Every detail of the vision retains its precision and clarity long after your vision journey has come to a close. You will find after you have had a vision that life often takes the route of your vision and because of your prior knowledge, you will act upon what you have seen and heard naturally. You will be prepared in a way you would not have been if you had connected to the Energy Source and witnessed the overlap and parallel nature of time. Many two leggeds in the modern world call visions premonitions, but the title is of no consequence, so long as you journey to the vision plane and understand the energy connection is at its most powerful in the vision state. Before I take you upon a Vision Journey Ceremony and share some people's vision experiences, I believe some examples of dreams will help differentiate between dreams and visions.

I will begin with a man who managed to overcome psychological scars from an abusive past with the help of dreams. I will call him Talk in Whispers. He said that he would not be able to participate in a Vision Journey Ceremony because he felt too frightened. I asked him, 'What do you fear so much?'

Talk in Whispers looked embarrassed and finally said, 'I have a recurring dream or vision, a dream I think, because it is repetitive and I never get anywhere near the Energy Source you speak about. In this dream, I feel terrible, so frightened, and I end up screaming until I wake myself up.' The man had beads of sweat on his forehead when he finished. I asked him to tell me more about the dream and he obliged, 'I am surrounded by a group of boys, they are about fourteen years old, but I am the age I am now, in my

thirties. There are about five of them and I know they intend to hurt me. I back away and start running, but they chase after me. I run without seeing and end up cornered. They crowd in on me, laughing at my terror. I feel powerless and just as they press forward, almost against my face, I start shouting and screaming, before I wake up, mercifully.' It had obviously taken a lot of courage for Talk in Whispers to tell me about his dream. He looked exhausted, but also a little relieved as he leaned over the back of a chair. I waited for a while and then I asked, 'Do you understand why this dream comes to you?' He shook his head and then sat down on the chair. He looked at me and said, 'I know you would call it a helper or a friend, not a nightmare, but from where I crouch cornered, it does not feel like any friend.' I asked the Energies to help me as Talk in Whispers needed guidance and healing.

He had to unravel the trapped fear that pushed forward in dreams. The fear remains imprisoned within him because the dream guide inspired further terror in Talk in Whispers and he was not ready to deal with it alone.

Talk in Whispers asked, 'Is there anything that can help to stop the dreams?' Talk in Whispers wanted to heal and that was the first step towards recovery. I nodded, 'Only you can stop the dreams. You are the energy power for yourself, I can only assist.' Talk in Whispers spoke nervously, but with determination, 'What do I have to do?' I smudged the area, Talk in Whispers and myself, then I asked him to close his eyes and relax. Then we journeyed back in time to a period when Talk in Whispers felt most vulnerable and frightened. I could see his eyes moving rapidly behind his closed lids. I reminded him to breathe deeply and that he was in a safe place.

Finally, Talk in Whispers was able to tell me that he had been badly bullied at school. It became so intolerable that he left school early without taking any of the examinations he knew he could have passed easily. Talk in Whispers believed that there was no-one he could turn to; although he had spoken to his parents and teachers, they seemed powerless to stop it. During that period in his young life, Talk in Whispers lost trust in his peers and, most important of all, he stopped trusting himself.

Talk in Whispers was still stuck in a time period more than seventeen years ago when he was a young teenager. He had not moved on with his life or regained his own power and energy connection. Talk in Whispers had to deal with the past, before he could embrace the present. Talk in Whispers was reluctant to talk in detail about what had happened, but eventually he conceded, 'I have blocked it out, I deliberately never thought about it again after leaving school. It was the worst time of my life and after it was over, I just wanted to live normally.' Talk in Whispers drank a glass of water and fell silent.

He could not live normally or connect truthfully with a free spirit until he managed to accept and then forgive, not condone, what had happened. Talk in Whispers said, 'I can't believe that it is still with me, I really thought I had forgotten all about it. I suppose you are going to tell me that is what my recurring dream was trying to help me with?' I nodded and he asked, 'Where do I go from here?' I answered, 'The dream will come again, this time, face your attackers and do not corner yourself. Take back your energy power and they cannot hurt you. You are older and wiser, they are still in the infancy of energy connection.'

I met Talk in Whispers about six months later and he said, 'I did not realize you could change a dream once you are in it. I stood up to them in the dream, although the dream came back a few more times until I realized I had not forgiven them. I managed to forgive, it was a difficult thing for me to do, but I did forgive about three weeks ago. I have not had the dream since.' Talk in Whispers reclaimed his own energy power with a little help from a recurring dream.

◄

Needing to Run Woman felt tense and angry, but fear and sadness lay just beneath the curt surface. It was late fall and the cold bite of winter was already stinging the noses of the four leggeds. It was bitterly cold outside and snow was not far off.

Needing to Run Woman said she had had this vision or dream before.

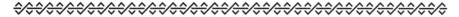

She said she could not tell if it was a dream or a vision, but it felt like a nightmare. I asked her, 'Where do you journey?' She replied, 'I do not go anywhere at all. I stay in my bed, but unfortunately, I am visited by a ghost or whatever you would call it.' Needing to Run Woman's brow furrowed into deep, dark lines as she spoke. Needing to Run Woman had a strong energy, but confusion and imbalance disturbed the natural flow. Needing to Run Woman said she wanted to be shown something she considered peaceful and wonderful when she slept, but she did not know exactly what that would entail. Suddenly, she burst into tears and spoke with a torrent of pent-up emotions, 'I had a terrible relationship with my father in life. I still feel it is totally unresolved, even though he is dead now. My father, or his spirit, comes to me every night. His shadow figure looks so tall and intimidating. He stands at the end of my bed and signals for me to go with him. I feel so scared and I do not want to go with him. Then I feel guilty and think I have let him down as he disappears.' 'Where do you think he wants you to go?' I asked. 'I don't know, maybe to the grave. I have never visited the grave since the funeral.

'Maybe he wants me to lay some flowers or make a semblance of peace. I am too frightened to question what he wants from me, because then I might have to talk to him and there are still too many bad memories.'

I waited as Needing to Run Woman tried to hold back her tears. I asked, 'If your father's energy continues to come in dreams, do you not think that he is trying to mend the past?'

Needing to Run Woman replied, 'I suppose he is. I guess I know that's what he is trying to do, but I am not sure if I am ready. A part of me wants to make peace and there's another part of me that does not know where to begin. It's not as if I ever really knew him properly, it was always so strained between us.'

The first soft drops of snow powdered the ground and soon the world turned white. Needing to Run Woman stared out of the window, 'I am struggling. I want to make amends as well, it could not have been just his fault; we just clashed. It was impossible for us to get along in life, maybe we can sort it out between life and death. There was no way I could have any sort

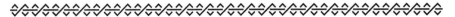

of reconciliation with him when he was alive. It seems a shame it has to be that way.'

It may have been Needing To Run Woman's sadness or sense of loss regarding her father–daughter relationship that created her dreams. The dreams were likely to continue as long as she felt antagonistic or guilty about her father. Needing to Run Woman had to learn to forgive herself and then her father before her pathway to the vision world would be revealed.

The snow fell harder and all signs of the footsteps of those who had walked were covered in sheeted white snow. Needing to Run Woman said, 'I came hoping for a quick answer, but I guess that was not realistic.

'It looks as though it may be a slow process as I learn to rethink a whole lifetime of feeling unhappy about the awkwardness and many misunderstandings between my father and myself. I do not know if the dream will come again, but maybe it has already given me the insight I needed.'

Needing to Run Woman had to decide how to take her first step towards recovery. The psychological scars would only heal when she was ready to allow them to and as she left, I believed, her dreams would not continue for too much longer. Needing to Run Woman and I joked as she waved and walked away into the deepening snow.

The snow took away the edges of the trees and shrouded Needing to Run Woman in its cleansing energy as her steps were blotted and covered with snow as she walked away.

◄

It was a warm summer's day. I decided to talk to Dancing Claw outside on the land, near the river; inviting nature's energy to help rebalance all those that needed healing. Dancing Claw sat uneasily on a tree stump. I asked her why she had come to see me. She spoke in short, worried sentences and kept brushing a strand of persistent red hair off her face. 'I have so many nightmares, almost every night. They are always about the same thing. The scenery is usually different in each one, but the action is the same.' I waited for her to tell me more. She spoke again, 'I am being perpetually chased by a man who, I believe, wants to hurt me.'

The river shone golden in the sunlight and reflected the woman's face. I waited for her to speak, but after some time, I broke the silence by asking her, 'Would you like to tell me about the last dream?' Dancing Claw looked up suddenly, but her eyes were on my left ear as she spoke, 'The last night-mare?' I nodded. 'Well, it was only last night. They are always very vivid and detailed. I was in a nightclub with two friends. One of my friends left and went to look for another friend, Cathy, a girl I do not like. Then, I was by myself and walked into one of the dancing rooms. The nightclub had four levels of dancing floors. There was a man staring at me as I walked into the room. He was wearing black leather trousers and an open-necked, white shirt. His hair was shiny, black and curly.

'I felt so uncomfortable in this man's presence and I felt his intentions towards me were bad. I left the room quickly and he did not follow me. I looked behind me several times to make sure he was not coming after me.

'Then Cathy appeared, she was with the same man I had just seen, but he had removed his shirt. I knew he wanted to hurt Cathy, I felt as though I could read his mind. I called her over and pretended to wipe messy lip-stick off her face. I whispered to her, 'That man is not to be trusted.' Cathy looked confused, then terrified as she looked at the man. The man stared at me coldly. He knew I had told Cathy that she needed to be careful. Then the man made a phone call.

'I took the opportunity to grab Cathy's hand and run while he was on the phone. We raced downstairs, but the black stairs seemed endless. Some-how, Cathy and I separated and I saw our other friend running towards the car park, where she had left her white van. Then I ran towards the car park, but the road was so desolate between there and the nightclub. I thought if he catches me here, there will be no-one to help me and he will harm me.

'Finally, I reached the car park, but it was empty. I ran on again, nearly blind with fear and panic. I saw the white van, but my friend was not there. I jumped inside the van and hid.

'When I dared to look up, I could see my mother and my cousin, Lizzy, walk past. Their faces were serious and worried. I wanted to call out to

them, but I was too afraid. I looked around and saw a black sports car parked only two spaces away from the van.

'I knew the sports car belonged to the man. My heart was pounding against my chest like rocks thrown at a wall. I felt faint and dizzy with fear. Then, inexplicably, the van swung around and crashed into the sports car. The man jumped out and he was furious. I pulled an old blanket over my head and tried to keep perfectly still. After a short time, I could not bear the thumping in my chest and I climbed out of the van.

'The man was waiting for me as I got out, but then he did not seem to recognize me. I ran in the opposite direction as fast as I could. I kept running and running into the night and when I woke, as always, I was covered in sweat and terrified. I feel so alone when I wake up, but often, I am too frightened to even turn on the light.'

Dancing Claw locked and unlocked her fingers as she spoke, but when she finished, she held her hands tightly on her lap, staring at the ground. I asked her, 'How do you feel once the fear has subsided?' She never raised her eyes, 'I feel shocked that I have had such a scary dream and confused as to why I should have nightmares like that.' I questioned her further, 'Why do you think you are being chased?' She thought about it for a few seconds, 'I really do not know. I do not know the man in real life and I cannot remember seeing anyone that fits his description especially.

'I am afraid that this dream is a premonition of something bad that could happen in the future.' I responded, 'Yet, nothing bad happens to you in the dream. You run away, but you are safe. You are never even caught by this man because when he sees you, he does not recognize you.'

Dancing Claw frowned, 'I know that I do not get hurt in the dream and I am not fearful of men. I am married and have a lovely, baby son. When I wake up, the man does not seem that important, but I feel a solid mass of fear inside that I cannot shake for at least half an hour.' I asked, 'If it is not the man you are afraid of, then why are you running away?'

She raised her voice, 'I feel as though I am running to save my life, but I do not know what I am running from really. That's strange not to know even when there is so much terror inside me.' I asked, 'Why do you not turn around and defend yourself?' She faced me for the first time, 'Because I am too afraid, I don't feel strong enough to deal with whoever or whatever is chasing me.' I paused for a moment, 'Do you feel that you could be running from yourself?'

Dancing Claw stared at me, 'Why would I run from myself? It is not as though you can out-run yourself is it? I shook my head, 'Women are much stronger than they realize, especially in dream-time or in visions. If you go into that dream state again, you might want to turn around and see what is behind you. If there is nothing, ask yourself in the dream why you are running away and the answer may come to you easily.

'So many women have lost touch with the energy connection. The power of the woman is incredible. Women help to balance the earth, but only when they have balance inside themselves first.'

Dancing Claw said, 'If I am running away from myself, then these dreams are even more frightening. I find it hard to believe that I have that much fear inside me, especially of myself. In a way, some of it makes sense and in another way, it seems surreal.

'Dreams are like that, though, so real at the moment of dreaming, even the most bizarre facts seem quite normal. It is only when you wake up that you realize, most of what you have dreamt is not possible in real life.' I smiled, 'The spirit and energy are capable of many things, it is only the physical body and modern society as we know it that prevent us believing what we are shown in the dream and vision state.'

Dancing Claw laughed, 'I want to remain firmly in this society. I feel safe here and I do not enjoy the experiences of dreams usually, especially that one.' I said, 'The dream is giving you the opportunity to look at yourself and the fears inside you. You will not be allowed to ignore them, because the fear has become part of your subconscious make-up. It is up to you when and how you decide to deal with it. Dreams are more gentle teachers than you realize and you are never given more than you can handle.

'The dreams will help you if you allow them to and are prepared to work on what is causing them.' I put my hand into the chilled river water and pulled out a red stone, 'This river stone's energy can help you face the fears, to face yourself.' Dancing Claw took the stone, but looked unsure, 'How can a river stone help me?' I smiled, 'If you feel you want to regain your own energy connection, look at the river stone. It has kept its own balance in the water and its energy is connected directly to the Source. Everything is living and we are all related.'

Dancing Claw put the stone in her pocket and returned my smile, 'I feel I am a long way from what you are saying, but there is obviously something out of balance inside of me, at least when I am dreaming; I am fine during waking hours. I will try to look at my fear when I dream again. I feel nervous about it, but I want the dreams to stop, so I am going to have to make a stand.'

We have the choice to continue on the same negative dream pattern or we can choose to heal. Dreams are persistent and challenge us to deal with inner, psychological problems. Dreams can also be seen as a prelude to the vision world. The nature of dreams as illustrated can be healing and preparatory for vision teachings. When dreams are interpreted correctly and accepted, it is time to release them and move onto the next natural phase of spiritual enlightenment; the vision world. The following is a vision journey ceremony I utilize to help people get in touch with their vision power and inner gifts.

Vision Journey Ceremony

Before beginning the ceremony, I offer tobacco to the Creator, the Energies and the four directions. Then the room is smudged with sacred sage smoke. The smudging includes all the people present in the sacred area. Then we are ready to begin our vision journey. I ask each person to find a comfortable place to lie upon the floor. It is best to use a blanket for warmth as the body temperature drops as the vision journey begins.

I ask each person to breathe in a calming, peaceful breath, hold the breath for a few seconds and then slowly exhale. Continue breathing in this way, until the body and mind relax.

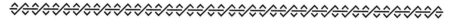

I say, 'You will begin to feel comfortable and your breathing will become quieter and deeper. As you lie still, feel your spirit rise up from your body. Remain relaxed and gentle with yourself, your spirit energy will return to your resting body once its journey is complete.

'As your spirit rises, watch it with your inner eye and heart-energy as it quietly floats a few feet above you, then higher and higher until you find a window or a door, and allow your spirit to go out through the opening. As your spirit moves out of the physical boundaries, go with it, leaving your reposed body behind for the moment. Allow the spirit energy to move upward outside the room and become part of grandfather sky. Your energy is rich with the blueness of grandfather sky and you utilize its energy to send you to where you need to go.

'Float over chimneys, buildings, fields and rivers until you reach the sea. Your energy spirit slides down a cliff like a feather blowing effortlessly in the wind. You are weightless. You are upon a beach. The sea is connected to the Energy Source as are all living things. This is your vision journey, your energy is powerful and free, allow it to take you wherever you need to go.'

I sing a sacred song to help prepare those who lie within the sacred space for the rest of the vision journey. I pray from the heart and ask for protection and guidance for all who journey into the vision world. The body must remain comfortable and feel light upon the floor. I say to them, 'Call upon the Creator, the Energies and all the ancestors to help guide you upon your spiritual voyage. As relaxation deepens, the mind grows quieter and there is less noise inside your head.' I sing another sacred song as the vision energy goes out to meet the spirit energy.

I am silent for approximately one hour and when the visions are over, I ask the spirit energy to journey back to the physical bodies again. It goes down through the top of the head, until the warmth reaches the toes. I ask each person to remain in a relaxed position, breathing gently for another ten minutes. Then they are ready to sit up slowly and, if they choose, they can share the vision. Tobacco is offered in gratitude for the vision. The area and participants are smudged once more before the room is vacated. These

are some of the visions the participants of the Vision Journey have chosen to share.

◄

One of the women who went on the Vision Journey felt perturbed by what she had seen. I will call her Wings Far. This woman was drawn into a red flamed sky. She asked the Energies to guide her away from the scorching heat, but her energy-spirit moved closer to it. Wings Far said, 'I was engulfed in the flames, but they did not burn, although it felt hot.

'I was sucked deeper into the fiery sky and I wanted to free myself from the overwhelming redness. Then my spirit was tumbled into a dark hole that split the scarlet space. I felt afraid, but I could not go back, I felt compelled to go on. I knew I was travelling within the darkness, but at the same time, I did not move. I surrendered to the blackness and even began to feel comforted by its nothingness. Then there was a sudden blast of wind, it sounded like a rising storm and I was lifted out of the hole and thrown into a pink-grey dawn. My energy became part of the new day and my own spirit was seen as colour. The greyness lifted and the pink gave way to a soft butter yellow. I felt totally free until I saw the dark hole and brilliant red sky moving towards me.

'They were mixed together like a cocktail. I tried to move away, but they hurtled ever faster and something was pushed into my hand. When I looked at my hand, there was a large green leaf lying on my palm. It smelled like toasted almonds and I closed my hand around it. As I did this, there was a wave of energy and I was back in this room.'

Wings Far asked me how I would interpret her vision. I felt it was a powerful energy vision that symbolized the damage grandfather sky has endured. Her energy-spirit had connected with the paternal guardian of all living things.

It could be seen as a sign that her help was needed to heal the damage done. The leaf was one of the many healing gifts provided by Mother Earth to help heal all living things.

Wings Far had already told me that she meditated and prayed for world peace and healing for Mother Earth. Her prayers and compassion had connected her to the Energy Source. I felt she would be shown more on the vision plane that would guide her to her ultimate pathway. I have met Wings Far on several other occasions since her Vision Journey ceremony and she continues to journey to the vision world. Wings Far has confirmed that her pathway is being slowly drawn in vivid colour by the Energies and that she is about to embark upon a new way of earth walking. Wings Far works as a herbalist. She also utilizes colour therapy to help heal the two leggeds and four leggeds, and sends energy to help heal Mother Earth.

◂

One Feather is a man whose vision led him to solid ground on top of a heather mountain. This was his place of safety, but even the mountain could not dilute the fear his visions placed in his heart. He wanted to know if he could change his own destiny. One Feather fervently believed in the omnipotence of fate. I responded, 'That depends. I believe some destinies are difficult to change, there are others that are quite flexible and yet other destinies that you can alter a great deal. Do you want to change your destiny?'

One Feather sighed, 'I believe I have been shown my destiny, but I do not understand. I am confused. I don't know.' He looked at me and hesitated before continuing, 'When I went on the Vision Journey ceremony, I had a vision. It is the same vision I have had before.

'I have also seen the spirit of an old woman during waking hours since I was about six or seven years old. This old woman has never spoken, just looked at me. She has appeared just about everywhere, even in my classroom. Then, when I was twenty years old, the old woman disappeared and I started to have these visions when I went to sleep at night.

'I call them visions and not dreams because I have had hundreds of dreams, and these visions are totally different. In my visions, and the same thing happened during the Vision Journey ceremony you helped prepare us for, I leave my body and I can see my sleeping, physical body, but I have risen above it. I am unconcerned about it, because I know it is safe and that I will return to it. During the Vision Journey ceremony, my spirit went on this long, power-dusty road as it always does when I am in visions. The energy looks and feels like a very soft, dense-white mist.

'I feel as though I am floating and when this feeling ceases, I am underwater, but I can breathe naturally, with less movement than a fish. There is warm, wet sand underneath my bare feet and I can hear a crashing and falling sound in the distance. I am totally relaxed and feel love for everyone and everything around me. I drift towards a large seashell and speak to a fish, but the fish just moves away.

'I am searching for someone or something, but I cannot find it. I continue to look and find myself rising out of the water onto the shoreline. There is a magnificent whale, but he is beached.

'I skim over the water until I reach him and I ask him, "Why are you taking your own life?" He opens his heavy eyes with great effort and answers slowly, "Because it is my life to take." I ask him again, "But why?" He closes his eyes and I turn to go, believing he is dead, but he speaks again, "I have lived long enough to see the bottom of the sea become the top of the earth. I have seen many creatures that belonged to the ocean give themselves up and shun the salty waters. They make sacrifices of themselves so man can have milk in his diet and red meat on his table. I have watched while the big trawlers ploughed through our clean waters and dirtied it. I have seen the men on board harpoon the biggest and best of us. I have seen fish and mammals ready to give new life, but their babies are torn out of their bellies. This I have seen and much more than my last few breaths will allow me time to tell.

' "The dolphins keep trying to talk to man and man takes their friendliness as a sign that these half-human beings can be exploited, captured and punished until their natural instinct to frolic and play is a tragic farce for the paying public. If they refuse to perform, they are served as an expensive delicacy. To die, as I wish, and at my own bidding, is not so bad

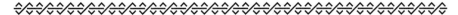

after all." The great whale laid its gigantic head upon the stony shore and passed away.

'At this point in the vision, I start to panic and run back into the sea, but the water is no longer my friend and it pushes itself into my lungs. I cannot breathe and feel as though the hostile, dirt-green waters will overpower and drown me. I am being crushed by a terrible watery weight. As I begin to fall down into the bottle-black depths of the ocean, I feel a hand reach out and pull me further into the abyss. I am too tired to fight as I am dragged downwards.

'Total darkness, like I have never known, blinds me. The hand has gone. I am alone and I am afraid. A voice comes out of the darkness, it is the voice of a woman. It is an old woman's voice and she whispers, "The darkest moment is always before the brightest spark." Then there is nothing but a graveyard quiet. The eerie silence and inky blackness terrify me, I want to shout for help, but I know that nobody can hear me at the bottom of the sea. I crawl on all fours, hoping to feel some inanimate object that might offer me some solidity, familiarity and hope in what I believe is my dying hour.

'The old woman's voice returns, "Why do you not speak?" I am too petrified to answer, but the voice insists, "Speak to me." I answer hesitantly, "What do you want from me?" The voice laughs, "What do *you* want from you? You have eighty-four years on this planet called earth, what do you want for sixty of these? After that, your spirit will leave, but your body is stubborn and will refuse to follow."

'I want to cry, but can't. The voice comes again, "Do you know where you are?" I do not answer and the voice quivers as it speaks, "You need light. Turn on the light sea-sun and let the two legged see the ancient world." A brilliant purple light opens up a hidden universe of glistening, lilac-tinted beauty. It looks like an illuminated piece of earth that resembles a sprawling, purple garden.

'I want to laugh with relief. I ask the voice, "Why have you brought me here?" The voice answers, "You came of your own free will. The Energies heard the sorrow in your words as you asked for enlightenment and guidance." I cut in, "But, this is not what I want, I mean, not what I expected." The voice replied, "What did you expect? What the two leggeds say they want is hardly ever what they need. You can stay here and learn more or you can go back to your earth dwelling." I ask to go back to earth without hesitation. The female voice laughs, "You will no sooner be back there than you will wish you were here again. This is the way of many mortals. You will come again, your destiny lies within this sea-world and that will bring you here again and again. One day you will accept this and stay. Go to the mountain and you will find your way back home. Before you go, wrap some seaweed around your heart to help heal your pains."

'I take a piece of floating seaweed and I fold it around my chest. I feel light-headed, but very relaxed. I enjoy the sensation and feel at peace before I am sitting on the same mountain I always return to before I wake up. When I am conscious again, I am back in my bed. I am breathing hard and feel my own sweat scalding my eyes.

'I grab a white cotton sheet that is often thrown on the floor during my vision and wipe my wet face. Several nights can go by and I am free of the vision, but it always returns and repeats itself with one or two variations. I am given the choice to go back or stay, and I always choose to come back. I wondered if the same vision would happen during this Vision Journey ceremony and it has. I cannot ignore this any longer, but I do not understand what it is trying to tell me or what I am meant to do about it.'

One Feather turned his head to face me and I could see confusion in his dark blue eyes. He spoke again, 'What frightens me most is that the vision starts off so easily with wonderful warmth and security, but ends in a wild, no-man's sea-world.' I nodded, 'You understand that this is a vision, a persistent one and the Energies are eager to show you something. You have already connected with the message that you are being given, now you must ask yourself if you are ready to understand it. It seems that you have been told the amount of years you will spend on Mother Earth, but that could be changed if you work with your own energy and decide to alter it.' One Feather interrupted, 'Yes, I understand that, but what does it all mean? I know destiny is the agreement we make before we come to earth, but what

are they trying to tell me? What am I supposed to do? I cannot take on sea pollution single handed, can I?'

I smiled, 'All things are possible. In order to complete, you must at some point begin. Many two leggeds have done remarkable work with little or no assistance to begin with, then later on once the energy gathers momentum other people join the magnetic force. Is this what you believe your vision is guiding you towards; sea cleansing and purification?'

One Feather shook his head, 'I believe it is. I feel deep inside me that this seems to be the answer, but I am not sure if I want to accept that. It seems too overwhelming and too difficult. It is not what I studied and I do not relish returning to college to do another totally unrelated degree.' I laughed, 'All things are related, but that is not necessarily obvious at first. This is not about the amount of time or work that you will have to put in, it is a question of whether you want to do this and if your energy is prepared to feel inspired and totally committed. It is a big undertaking and if you do not feel that your heart is in it, then you will not be able to overcome the many obstacles that you will encounter along the watery pathway.'

One Feather looked more anxious than ever and I suggested that he might want to offer a pinch of tobacco to the Creator, the Energies, the Four Directions and to the sea before going to bed that night. I heard from One Feather again within a short period of time and his spirit was much lighter. He said, 'A lot of things in my waking hours have led me back to my vision, although not to the bottom of the sea, but nearly! I laid out the tobacco and made my offering, I also prayed for more information and guidance. In a vision that night following the vision journey ceremony, I was taken to where all human life began underneath the water in cell form.

'The energy was incredible as I saw our ancient ancestors, before we were earth bound. I have been told that our greatest source of energy and inspiration is always in our first home, but many people do not know their first home or even their last one. I was told that the sea still calls to many people today, all landed, but still connected through energy to the sea. I am one of the people the sea beckons to and, as I said, my waking steps have led me to it. I am ready to take on the challenge and I no longer feel trapped by uncertainties or overwhelmed by the enormity of the task. I am not concerned about my life span, but I am concerned about what I do with the earth years I have been given.' I listened carefully and felt my energy circle as he spoke the language of the Old Ways. His visions had helped guide him on his pathway. One Feather gave a wry smile, 'My life will never be the same again, but it might be much better.'

◄

Sun Fire Sitting told how his Vision Journey took him to a sacred tree. He sat in front of the tree waiting for a sign, but only the wind blew upon his face and he could not read its meaning. The landscape had many secret omens, but his mind blinded his spirit and he could not interpret the code.

Then Sun Fire Sitting spoke, 'I thought, why am I in this vision, when I do not understand it. I did not want to sit in front of the tree forever. I wanted to walk away, but there was only desert sand every side of me and I felt some degree of protection from the tree. It offered a cool shade from the rising sun.

'Then the sun bore down on me until beads of sweat salted my mouth and I felt dizzy. I believed the sweltering blaze of the sun would set the tree alight and destroy my only respite from the blistering heat. My chest was stung with sharp pains and my body was lifted from the roasting sand. I was held mid-air. The sun tore into my skin and scorched the hairs on my arms. My legs dangled just above the ground. I tried to cover my face, but my hands were clasped immovably to my sides. At that point, I believed the sun would fry me. I had given up hope and surrendered to the blaze when my body moved of its own volition and gravitated towards the tree. The chilled leaves brushed against my body as I reached it and offered some comfort for an instant, before the bark retreated as my body was moved out towards the sun again. I was danced in and out from the tree until my senses were numbed and I was no longer able to think coherently.

'As my mind was dulled, feelings of pain, fear and despair lessened. I could not struggle or gain any form of control. The sun had won and I was ready to splinter into its rays. At this time, the heat meant nothing to me and the pain disappeared. I was aware that my body continued its ritualistic dance, but my spirit had left its confined suffering.

'My spirit travelled up towards the sun and I embraced its powerful heat without fearing its indomitable strength. As I rose ever closer to the sun, I felt the natural world beneath worship and revere the yellow life above its head. The sun touched my spirit and melted it within its flames. White heat became my spirit's life force and I did not want to leave its potent, hot medicine.

'The sun consumed my spirit. I had no desire to return to earth or to the magnetic tree, but the earth shouted my name. My name echoed around the sun until it penetrated my spirit.

'I could not ignore the earth's call and the sun opened its rays and I was dancing in and out towards the tree again. The dance felt different, I needed the heat and not the shade of the tree. Then, the dance stopped and I lay upon the welcome blaze of the sand. My spirit drifted again and when I woke up, I was in this room.'

Sun Fire Sitting had described what many Plains Native Americans nations practised in search of spiritual truth and guidance; the Sun Dance. The Sun Dance entailed days of offerings, fasting, dancing and singing before chest piercing by an experienced medicine man. The Sun Dancer ceremonially honoured the pain and heat as a vision was sought. Sun Fire Sitting felt he might have to go through a Sun Dance, but I believed he had already gone through the ceremony in the vision world of energy. There was no need to endure a physical Sun Dance. Sun Fire Sitting's energy had become one with the energy of the sun and he could call upon its power. The heat is a great healer and Sun Fire Sitting received the most effective heat medicine during his vision.

◄

Sees Beyond felt his energy leave the room as soon as a yellow light appeared. He said, 'My spirit was floating and then circling at the top of the

room until it disappeared into a bright yellow light. I was pulled by an invisible hand into a mountainous region. There were caves hidden behind caves with hardly any room for me to walk.

'The track between the city of caves was broken and twisted. I tripped and fell several times, but my spirit was pulled forward and I could not stop. I was compelled to keep going. It is difficult to explain.

'I stopped outside a small cave. The entrance was narrow and close to the ground, just a little bigger than a badger's sett. I knew I had to go inside, but I felt nervous about lying on my stomach and wriggling in. It was not only the physical effort of getting in, but something told me that once I was inside, it might be difficult to get out again. I stood outside the cave opening for what seemed like a long time, then I had to go in and I even wanted to go inside. I wriggled flat on my stomach and sharp-edged stones cut my legs as I dragged them into the darkness after me.

'It was pitch black inside, but the blackness felt strangely warm. I put my hands out and something scratched against them. I quickly pulled back and felt wet blood on the back of my hand. The blood dripped onto a stone and echoed loudly around the cave dwelling. A light flickered against the stone streaked pinkish red with my blood. I dropped to the ground and tried to use the stone's light to see my damaged hand.

'My hand was lost between shadow and light, but even when I moved my hand right in towards the faint stone light, I could not see a cut or any sign of blood. I felt my hand, but there was no abrasion and the wetness had disappeared. I was about to stand up when my eye caught sight of something shimmering on the wall.

'The stone light dimmed and enough natural light filled the cave for me to see what was hanging on the wall. I felt as though I was in the dark hallway of an ancient house.

'When I reached the wall, I could discern that the hanging was made of deerskin. There were symbols of various red and black hues painted or imprinted upon the rectangular cut piece of deerskin. The skin smelt stale, but the scent of deer was unmistakable. The symbols showed two men fighting. There was a volcano in the middle and the same two male figures

joined hands on the other side of the volcanic explosion. There were birds that I believed to be eagles and thunderbirds and other animals I could not recognize or name. There was a picture of two suns in red placed centrally at the top and bottom of the picture. There was also the figure of a woman with her arms spread upward as if in prayer to the sun placed near the top. There were pictures of trees and leaves at each corner of the skin.

'As I stared at the symbols in semi-darkness, everything blurred and I was outside the cave sitting on a large rock. A deerskin was stretched on the rock and a man was mixing colour. There were no symbols on the deerskin. The man began to paint the deerskin. As he painted, he explained the symbolism to me.

'I was told that the deerskin symbols contained knowledge passed down by a people from another time and place. It showed two suns that represented the two worlds the original people inhabited. The fighting men depicted the beginning of war that destroyed everything, but it returned to life and there was peace again.

'The thunderbirds and eagles symbolized the spiritual pathway and energy of the sacred birds. The thunderbird was also an example of a sacred winged one who had become extinct. The man said, "Extinction is possible for all of us alike if we are not prepared to take responsibility and greater care of this planet." The woman with outstretched arms was Mother Earth appealing for help. The trees and healing leaves were the life force that held the earth together, but they were scattered to the four directions as the world became increasingly unstable. The man stopped painting and I was inside the large, semi-lit cave again. The cave grew lighter as the sun poured into its shadowy caverns, and I was back in my body in this room again.'

Sees Beyond felt convinced that he was taken back in time by the vision world. He stared into the distance, 'I received knowledge from the most far-away past that makes me believe that many things are already set in place by us. There was a sense of pre-destination as well as the chance of changing our destructive course.'

I was reminded of the Apache's Sacred Prayer Chart. Long ago, all Apache medicine men had a medicine deerskin inscribed with ancient teachings and mythological symbolism. When the Apache medicine man wanted to connect with the power of the Great Spirit and the Energies, he would sit upon the deerskin.

The Apache medicine man would chant and sing sacred songs until his energy connected with the Energy Source that provided him with the wisdom and knowledge he sought. Sees Beyond had also received what his spirit required during the Vision Journey.

◄

Tree Talker was silent for a long time after her Vision Journey. When she finally spoke she said, 'I was walking in a forest. The trees were all different, I was aware of each personality. The grass was wet and slapped against my ankles as I walked. The air smelt fresh with pine and drenched wood. I kept walking without knowing where I was going. I felt safe and knew I was being guided. Dripping leaves showered lightly on my head and my hair stuck to my face. I wiped my eyes with the back of my hand and brushed away the wet hair. I stood still and waited. I did not know what I was waiting for, but I was compelled to be patient. I looked behind me and I saw a gigantic oak tree. It had lived for so many centuries that its bark had blistered and was rubbed raw from the rain.

'I touched its battered skin and the dust of ancient life vanished upon my fingertips. My eyes closed of their own accord and I felt the tree enfold my body and circle around my spirit. I became part of the tree. I could feel and breathe the tree's age-old wisdom and stand upon the immovable foundation of deeply embedded, strong roots.

'As the oak tree's branches swayed in the wind and bent under the weight of fresh rain, I was aware of other trees joining the dance that nature had provided for us.

'Colours ran through me and the inside of the oak was breathing and pulsating with hues of blue, red, green, yellow, pink and purple. The shimmering colours lapped in and out like the ebb and flow of the sea. I could see people from olden days worshipping the oak tree. The oak tree bestowed healing colour vibrations upon the people as they chanted and prayed.

'Generations ran into new generations and the tree energy helped to heal each person who touched it with respect and compassion. All passage of time ran into one dimension of life and the tree was the grandparent of all that breathed.

'The trees held a ringed record of all mankind from the dawn of human beings. I saw the most magnificent empires that rose and fell timelessly, yet within their own time frame that was ordained before their existence. I saw species come to life and become extinct, often through the erosive hand of man and the modern world. Then I saw similar animals return again, or their relations, in a slightly different form.

'The crystallization of many life cycles gelled into one circular grove of wood. Emerald-coloured memories emphasized the power of nature. The healing sensations of wood balm filled my spirit. Modern people walked past the tree and the tree's energy blew healing upon mankind as it had since the earth began. The tree's equilibrium was undisturbed and knowingly silent, even when many forests were desecrated. The trees understood that to slay them is to end life upon earth as they rejoin the Energy Source. As I accepted this, I was doused in vivid, bright lights and I felt my spirit rise to the top of the tree. The branches encircled me as I was lowered to the wet forest floor that covered my feet. The sun peeped out and a rush of air and light returned me to my own body. As I reentered the physical form, I felt my skin and hair dry on my way to this dimension.'

Tree Talker did not feel the need to ask what her journey represented because she already understood. Since then, we have met many times and she continues to talk to the trees, 'I lay my hands upon a tree, any tree, and I feel its life force. I ask it to help me and it always does, even if I do not understand the message immediately. I also give healing to injured or diseased trees. It is beyond my understanding why trees are mutilated and uprooted for economic gain and property development invasion. The balance of this planet is dependent upon the ecology of the trees: if that is taken away, we will all suffer the consequences.' I felt the energy of the grandparent trees respond to her wise words.

◀

Walks Far found it difficult to free her spirit at first. Then slowly it managed to leave the room and she travelled to a desert. The sun had burnt life out of all visible plants. She could only see fried and brittle stalks where plants might once have grown green. Walks Far thought that nothing could survive in such a wasteland. She said, 'I walked upon the scalded grains of sand and looked around from every angle, but there was nothing except the sky and sand. I thought that nothing could live in such a desolate burnt-out place and I also wondered why my spirit chose to travel to the hot emptiness.

'Although the heat was sweltering, and I was aware of that, I was not affected by it. My spirit body felt even and my temperature did not escalate with the unrelenting torch of the sun. I did not fight against my destination, I quietly thought there must be a reason for this that I cannot see or understand at this moment. I continued to walk with no idea where I was going. In fact, I felt as though I was walking to nowhere.

'A dusty image glittered and danced in the direction I was walking. At first I believed it was a mirage, but as the distance closed, a man came into sight. He wore a piece of red cloth wrapped around his waist and his hair was black and shoulder length. His skin was sun varnished to almost mahogany. I stood still and waited for the man to reach me, but as he came closer, his eyes did not meet mine and he walked past me. I hesitated for a moment, before following him.

'He walked for a long time and I continued to follow him about two feet behind his footsteps. Then he stopped and turned to look at me briefly, and he stooped down and picked up a handful of sand before walking on again. At this point I had to run to catch up. He stopped suddenly and as he turned towards me I noticed he was holding a small stone bowl in his hands. I had not seen it before. He held out the bowl and chanted towards the sun. Then he placed the handful of sand he had picked up earlier into the bowl. He sat down on the sand and laid the stone bowl beside him. I watched him as he dug deep into the sand,

about a foot below the surface. His hand returned filled with damp green leaves. He ground the leaves into the sand with a small, round pebble as he chanted again.

'When he finished chanting, he offered me the bowl and I understood that I must sample its contents, although I did not relish the idea of eating sand. I ate a pinch of the strange mixture which, surprisingly, did not taste that bad. The man nodded to me and ground the mixture together once more and then he left. This time, I knew I was not allowed to follow him and his image dissolved into the heat and the horizon.

'I sat upon the sand for a while longer. The man had taken the stone bowl, but a little of the mixture remained and I held it in my hand. It smelled like rain-fresh pine and that was peculiar to me in the blaze of the desert. Then my spirit lost the sensation of the hot sand and I was in this room again.'

Walks Far's vision had a sense of the Zuni nations' medicine men. The Zuni medicine men often ground sacred herbs and plants combined with mineral and mineral pigments in stone mortar bowls using a sacred pebble. The Zuni nation was renowned for their powerful medicine. Walks Far concluded, 'The full meaning of my vision journey will come to me in time and I want to wait until the sun is at its hottest.' Walks Far is still waiting for a greater understanding of what she was shown.

◄

Energy connection and freedom are strange concepts for many two leggeds today. So much that was free like the fresh air we used to breathe has been polluted and contaminated. We buy vaporizers and humidifiers to help fill our lungs without constricted throats. The freedom to run on the land has also been forbidden.

Lands have new owners other than Mother Earth and these owners have 'No Trespassing' signs everywhere. I wear my own sign and it is, 'We are not separate from the land or each other, we are all one energy and related'. Where can we find freedom these days? Look into your own heart, to the last frontier, the freedom to journey into the vision world. Reclaim what was

always yours and mine by birthright: the freedom to vision and talk to our greatest teachers, the Energies.

Visions take us by the hand and connect us to the Energy Source. Often in visions, we are shown sacred ceremonies, medicine, herbs and plants that will heal two leggeds, four leggeds, flying, swimming and crawling ones. The spiritual knowledge we are given can later be used on the physical plane to soothe, comfort and help heal the many diseases and imbalances within our material world.

I have been shown ancient herbal medicines and energy healing on the vision plane. Many Native Americans learned the medicine of the sacred herbs and plants from the four leggeds, but many were also given this vital knowledge in the vision world.

◄

8

Ancient Herb and Plant Healing

Everything on the earth has a purpose,
Every disease an herb to cure it,
And every person a mission.
This is the Indian theory of existence.
MOURNING DOVE (1888—1936), SALISH

Mother Earth opened her pores as grandfather sky purified the ancient herbs and plants. After the cleansing rainfall, the energy in the air sweetened. The intoxicating scent of sacred herbs and plants was carried upon the wind and spread a healing balm upon those in need. The days stretched a little longer with the widening of the sun. It was not yet night-time, but my energy drifted away from where I sat and soon I was upon the vision plane. My energy was taken back to a scene and a moment in time when the Great Grandfather Spirit and his great grandson journeyed together on the earth plane to collect herbal medicine.

I could see the Great Grandfather Spirit as he leaned over a brook. The young boy chewed a blade of grass as he watched his Great Grandfather fill a glass bottle with clean, fresh water from the brook. Spring echoed in every movement they made and laughter was in the air. My energy suddenly stilled and when it circled again, I was breathing the past, present and future. The infinity of time belonged to each second Mother Earth had existed. I felt at one with all living things.

The Great Grandfather was whistling as he finished bottling the cooling water. He had already prepared food for our journey. I felt that this journey had been taken on the well-worn hill trail many times before.

As this information assimilated, I could see the Great Grandfather and his great grandson riding together. The great grandson was only two summers at that moment as he sat on the front of the Great Grandfather's bay mare, No Shadow, as the Elder held him in his arms.

They were heading for the hills again. Healing sage called to them and its odour permeated the grassy track uphill. The young boy suddenly transformed into the age I had seen him before; nine summers, and in this accelerated passage of time, he rode upon his own horse, Ghost Walker. Ghost Walker was No Shadow's young foal some moons ago. I felt Ghost Walker pulling at the bit as he pawed the ground eagerly. Ghost Walker enjoyed the sage expedition as much as the two leggeds. I knew that Ghost Walker never took to a saddle. As the energy present faded, I could see the great grandson's father, who had helped Ghost Walker to learn to carry two leggeds, as the horse resisted each saddle he tried. The boy's father relented in the end and remarked with understanding, 'His spirit just won't carry the leather, he is a free horse, let him choose how he wants to help us.' The young boy never learned to ride with a saddle and stirrups. Ghost Walker taught him the strides of his body and they rode together for many long, happy years on the earth plane.

I could hear the Great Grandfather speak about the similarity between the young boy's horse and his own vision quest horse, Storm Runner. He looked skywards, 'We are all related, all living things, and the blood and energy keep flowing, even when we believe someone, something or a beloved four legged is gone, it is not, that spirit revives itself and finds its way back to us.'

As they rode out, I could hear the birds and other flying ones chattering like a band of two leggeds. The Great Grandfather said that they were preparing to feed their young and teach them the way of nature, 'Time for them to move camp will come in the fall and it will be bad medicine for them here after the sun disappears.' The horses walked their easy gait.

The horses knew their way and picked out their climb like the big horned sheep that grazed nearby. The Great Grandfather inhaled the sharp scent of the hill, 'Nothing changes on these hills. They have been the same before and will be the same after many small lives on Mother Earth have completed their journey. These are my friends, my friends who give us sage and other sacred plants and herbs. No-one could take these hills and there was no reason to gorge and plunder as no-one ever heard of yellow gold in these parts. Yet, there is gold here, but not the cold, hard metal glitter that drives two leggeds to use the darkest energy. There is gold of another texture and colour, it is soft and green and it has much greater value. It is the greatest gift and what is most needed by the two leggeds, four leggeds, flying, swimming and crawling ones.

'Here lies the gold to heal the badly diseased, the sick and the dying. Held in the arms of these hills lie many cures. Sage, cedar and osha, three of our healers are kept safe and protected here, waiting to give their help to those with a good heart. You need a pure, compassionate heart to pick sage and cedar or to dig for the osha root or for any other medicine you call

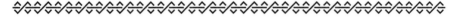

upon. You also need to understand the sacred herbs and speak their language. You must offer thanks and always perform the sacred ceremonies. The infinity of time is the infinity of healing.'

I felt the gratitude in the horses' hearts as they were allowed to graze. The horses picked up their heads from time to time as their tails brushed away swarming horseflies. Later, the horses watched with keen interest as the Great Grandfather carried out sacred herb and plant ceremonies. His prayers echoed in the hills.

I felt the youthful bounce in the great grandson's footsteps as he followed his Great Grandfather's steps to a selected plant. The young boy asked how his Great Grandfather knew which plant was willing to help. The Elder replied, 'My medicine friend calls me over and gives me permission to utilize its sacred healing powers.'

As the Great Grandfather picked the sage, he sometimes lowered his head in awe and reverence towards the plant before he spoke to the young boy, 'This is one of the greatest gifts from the Creator to the two leggeds and the four leggeds. Sage cleanses the air and brings good balance to all living things.

'The heart energy must be especially pure when picking sage. If ceremony and gratitude are not given when picking sacred medicines, then when the plant is taken away, it will be as dead and extinct as many mother tongues have become. Look closely and listen to this sage leaf, it will talk to you if you know how to listen.'

Then the Great Grandfather offered tobacco to the four directions until the sage plant was encircled in a red-brown ring. He laid his left hand just above the plant and began to sing a sacred song. His song became a spoken prayer, 'Great Spirit, Creator, look upon Mother Earth and have pity upon the humble two leggeds. They have forgotten how to give offerings and thanks. The language of plant energy is a mystery to them, help them to reconnect with themselves so that they may talk to their healing friends.' The Great Grandfather Spirit offered another large pinch of tobacco and the Elder and the young child waited.

The great grandson's eyes were fixed upon the sacred sage. After a few minutes, the pointed leaf of the sage touched the Great Grandfather's raised hand. The Great Grandfather rested his hand upon the leaf and smiled, 'It is happy to come with us. Did you hear it speak my young boy?' The young boy laughed with delight, 'I felt energy, like a gush of wind fly from the plant to us.' The Elder ran his hand through the young boy's hair, 'That is the healing energy of the sage plant. You have felt its energy now, later you will talk and listen to each other as you exchange energy. The sacred sage will teach you many things.'

Then the energy moved within me and large tobacco leaves surrounded us. The Great Grandfather held the tobacco in his hands as he raised his arms towards grandfather sky. The young boy raised his own arms as they prayed side by side. The Great Grandfather and his great grandson took deep breaths as they inhaled the sacred tobacco plant and the Great Grandfather asked the tobacco to share its powerful medicine with them. The Great Grandfather gently caressed a tobacco leaf as he spoke, 'Tobacco is like sage, the two leggeds were given this medicine many moons ago and it is a great gift. It allows the two leggeds to talk with the Creator and send their words and prayers in the channupa's sacred smoke. Many two leggeds do not understand what they have in their hands when they see the tobacco leaf and they pull it without regard and smoke it for the wrong reasons without prayer or ceremony. So the tobacco turns against them and diseases of humankind's own making take away the energy balance of the spirit, mind and body. I feel for my friend, the tobacco plant, because many bad words have been spoken against this healer.

'It is easy to blame the silent plant, as poisonous chemicals are poured upon its pure head. The two leggeds do not look at themselves and see what they have done to it and by the time they do, for many, it will be too late.'

Again, the Great Grandfather offered thanks, prayers and performed a sacred ceremony for the tobacco plant and the fertile land that grows it before he began to pick. When they had gathered enough tobacco leaves, the Great Grandfather Spirit made a low noise in his throat and No Shadow trotted over to him, followed by Ghost Walker.

My energy moved again and was as light as the scent of sweetgrass it followed. Its pungent fragrance drew upon my energy until I felt the dizziness

in the young boy's head. The Great Grandfather laughed, 'This sweetgrass is well named as it steals your heart through your nose. This seducer helps energy and wounded souls pass into the Spirit World and can even help them back to Mother Earth, although that journey is always much harder.' The Great Grandfather sat with his great grandson as they began to braid the sweetgrass, praying and singing happy songs. When they had completed their sweetgrass braids, the Great Grandfather wore one around his throat and he also wound a protective necklace around his great grandson's neck.

As time drifted into a higher sun, I watched as the Great Grandfather Spirit and the young boy raised their arms in prayer to the healing flat cedar tree. 'Flat cedar offers itself up easily,' but the Great Grandfather cautioned, 'It is easy to find cedar, but to find good medicine cedar depends upon the heart's ability to speak the tree energy.

'The cedar tree that is deep green in colour has the best medicine. Use all your senses, smell it and let it sting your nostrils as its energy goes straight to your own energy. Flat cedar can heal many imbalances. It pulls poison from the two leggeds and the four leggeds.

'There are more plants, herbs, roots and flowers on fruitful Mother Earth to help the two leggeds, four leggeds, flying, swimming and crawling ones than any two legged can name or remember. Even though so much knowledge has been forgotten, the power of the Energy Source remains open to those who are willing to connect. All things lost can be found in the circular energy of life.'

I felt my energy mingle with the roots of sacred osha under the earth as the Great Grandfather prayed as he dug. Old, wise hands lifted the osha from its hidden lair and the young boy's nimble fingers joined the Elder's as they asked the osha's permission to take some healing roots. The Great Grandfather Spirit spoke, 'The Creator knew that the two leggeds would need different herbs all the moons of the year, so he allowed cedar to be fresh and green for us all the days of our lives. Yet, other sacred plants and herbs come only at certain times of the year, when it is most likely they will be required by the two leggeds. Osha is one of those powerful herbs that springs to life in early summer. It is secretive, it has to be because not everyone has the right to dig for it. It lies hidden underneath the soft clay shaded beneath a leafy plant. Not many two leggeds in today's world have any knowledge about the sacred osha.

Maybe it is better this way as osha is an all-purpose medicine, but like tobacco, if it is abused, its medicine will turn into negative energy. During the time of the Old Ways, the two leggeds understood the power of osha. They gave the Great Spirit, the Energies and the osha root itself offerings and gratitude because the osha had made its home nourished in the rich soil of Turtle Island.

The bear, our four-legged friend, showed the two leggeds where the osha root grew and how it could heal the sick. The bear was honoured for teaching the two leggeds about the osha root and ceremonies were performed for the four legged. As time passed, the spiritual connection slowly severed and the Old Ways changed to material new ways, and it was then that the sacred osha root started to die away. What remains of this sacred root is hidden far in the forests and the leafy hills. The young boy's hands were darkened by the brown, damp clay that surrounded the osha root. The great grandson cleaned the osha root and looked at his Great Grandfather before chewing a little osha with a nod of permission from the Elder. The young boy wrinkled his nose as the root became increasingly bitter against his tongue. He wanted to spit it out, but the Grandfather shook his head, 'You must pray and swallow the sacred osha as it is a powerful healer. It can heal the brain and that is often the most difficult part of the two legged because it can confuse and distort the messages from the energy and the heart. The brain in many two leggeds has become blocked and the energy connection founders.'

The great grandson prayed quietly as he swallowed the osha. The Elder laughed at the young boy's relieved face. The Great Grandfather Spirit tousled the young boy's hair, 'Sometimes, what tastes sweet is not as sweet as it tastes and that which is bitter is not truly bitter.' The great grandson shared the Elder's laughter.

My own energy moved with the sacred plants and herbs, whilst still remaining with the energy of the Great Grandfather Spirit and the young boy. It was a feeling of completeness and being at one with all living things. As the sun began to disappear into the soft evening light, I was aware they had picked two full sacks of sage. The Great Grandfather repeated the same ceremony with each plant he picked. Some plants did not wish to be picked and their wishes were honoured with a separate ceremony for remaining upon Mother Earth. The Great Grandfather picked as much as he needed, making sure there was plenty left behind on each stem and root for re-growth and the plant's own survival needs. Then, he offered another large pinch of tobacco and thanked the plants for their generosity. 'Only ever take what you need and remember to leave many plants and herbs behind for the sacred plant and for other two leggeds, four leggeds, flying, swimming and crawling ones. It is time to ride back down the hill and we will burn some of this healing sage from the old hill. Afterwards the good spirits and energies will fill our home.'

My energy glided upon the ground towards the loose sage leaves as they dried in the sun. Then I was part of the Great Grandfather and the young boy's energy as they parcelled the sacred medicine into buckskin bags. Time flowed into another night and I felt the pain of a sick man approach the Great Grandfather's house.

The man's pain was so sharp it twisted his insides and he grasped his stomach in agony. His spirit paled with the excruciating stabs and he believed he would go to the Spirit World, although he did not feel ready to leave Mother Earth. The ailing man knocked upon the door and asked the Great Grandfather to help him. The young boy brought a bag of dried sage as his Great Grandfather requested and then the Elder began to pray.

The Great Grandfather Spirit placed ten sage leaves in his left hand and rolled them into a ball. The sick man lay wearily in a chair, occasionally watching the Elder roll another ball of sage. The man's eyes watered with pain as he clutched his right side. The Great Grandfather gently tipped one ball of sage onto a scallop shell and lit it. The soothing sage smoke filled the room. The Great Grandfather Spirit began to chant, shaking a rattle in one hand and holding the burning sage in the other. He circled the man sunwise, until wisps of sage smoke created long, sinewy figures that touched the man lightly and then disappeared. The Great Grandfather put the other ball of sage in some clear water, placed his hands around the glass without touching it, and continued to pray and chant.

When he had finished, he turned to the ailing man, 'Drink this my friend and pray for good health.' The man drank the water and the Great Grandfather gave him the wet ball of sage to take with him, 'When this ball of sage is dry, find a sacred burial spot and lay the sage there. This sacred spot must not be revisited, allow Mother Earth to help. If the Creator wishes you to live, I will see you again and soon. Use your own energy to help you and release all hard feelings, many are caught in your stomach.' The sick man recovered slowly as he learnt to work with his own energy, sacred herbs and plants.

Summer faded into tomorrow's summers as I saw the man return each season the sun was at its strongest. The man, now fit and healthy, would ask the Great Grandfather if he could have some more sage. The Great Grandfather waited for this man as he felt his energy approach. The Elder had already prepared a bag of sage for him.

I saw many two leggeds call upon the Great Grandfather Spirit who helped to heal them by connecting them with their own healing energy. The Elder also helped them to reconnect to the Energy Source. As the Great Grandfather gave the man one more healing and a bag of sage, my energy slipped from the vision plane and I woke up.

The sacred herbs were within my energy and I felt healing in every breath. I looked outside and I could see the wild mountain sage as its tips touched the skyline. There are many healing plants and herbs upon Mother Earth. There are as many healing herbs as there are ailments, diseases and imbalances.

Many of these herbs and plants can be mixed together depending upon the particular requirement and energy level of the person who is suffering. Within one single plant or herb there is a multitude of healing properties. I have listed below some of the herbs and plants most commonly used by Native Americans since ancient times. However, there are limitless other uses for the herbs and plants mentioned, either used by themselves or combined with other healing medicines. It must be appreciated that it is not only the herbal remedy in itself that heals a person, but it is essentially the person's own energy learning to rebalance and accept good health. Healing also depends upon the person's ability to reconnect and work with the Energy Source.

Healing Trees, Plants and Herbs

WARNING: ALL SACRED TREES, PLANTS AND HERBAL MEDICINES CAN ONLY BE ADMINISTERED BY AN EXPERIENCED MEDICINE PERSON

Native American medicine people utilized plants and herbs to heal. The natural medicine was administered in diverse ways. However, the most popular way to work with the herbal remedies was by mixing the herb or plant with a quart of boiled water until a healing, herbal tea was prepared. Herbal teas are still prepared in the same way and it is recommended to drink whilst the tea is hot. After the initial intake of tea, the medicine can be allowed to cool and thereafter it is possible to refrigerate and reheat it later, dependent upon the quantity required and the daily recommendation. This way the herbal tea can be taken over a period of days before a fresh brew is required. Normally, three cups a day is suggested: first thing in the morning before food, then a cup at midday and one before going to bed at night.

As stated, there are diverse methods and ways to utilize the healing herbs and plants, and I have listed particular medicinal practices in accordance with specific nations.

ALFALFA (BUFFALO HERB)

The buffaloes enjoyed the healing properties of the alfalfa as a nutritious food. The flowers of the plant were occasionally used in ceremony as a celebration of the buffalo.

The buffalo herb flowers were used as a medicine tea to help cope with exhaustion and listlessness. It was believed this buffalo herb tea invigorated those who felt tired and restored them with an energy not unlike the stamina of a buffalo.

This healing flower is rarely used today and the buffalo herds have long since vanished from the plains, although other four leggeds still enjoy the healthy taste of the alfalfa.

ASPEN

The Cree nation have honoured and given thanks to forest aspen since ancient times. The aspen was understood to have a direct spiritual link to the Creator and many prayed to the tree for guidance and strength.

The Cree nation understood the power and great beauty of the white-coated aspen and shared it with other two leggeds as a healing medicine. During the cold winter months, the aspen's inner bark was ground down into a fine powder and mixed with hot water to make medicine tea. It brought on sweats and healed fevers, bad colds and persistent coughs.

Today, the Cree nations continue to go out to the white forests and offer tobacco in thanks to the grandparent aspen for all the tree has done for them and their ancestors.

BLOODROOT

Many Native Americans felt the life-line blood connection between bloodroot and themselves. They included its sacred colour in various ceremonies and would often paint their faces scarlet red for protection before a battle. If the bloodroot is used for the wrong purposes, it can cause poisoning and it is not recommended as a body dye anymore.

The Rappahannock nation made a tea of the root of bloodroot plant and drank it to ease the pain of rheumatism and tired muscles. Some medicine

people of the Rappahannock nation deliberately induced vomiting with unusually large quantities of bloodroot tea if they believed the afflicted person was poisoned or his or her stomach was dangerously infected.

Bloodroot can be highly toxic and, like all sacred medicines, it must be honoured and understood. It is rarely used nowadays, but some Native American medicine people still seek it out when many other methods have failed.

BONESET

Almost every nation upon Turtle Island used boneset at one time or another. Boneset was honoured as a great spiritual gift to the two leggeds. It was placed centrally in some ceremonies, particularly if a medicine person was dealing with broken bones.

Boneset travelled with the Native American nations and was passed onto those who needed it. Boneset has one of the largest variety of uses and each nation worked with this sacred leaf in a different way. The Alabama nation used it to relieve stomach aches and the Iroquois and the Mohegans for fevers and colds. The Ojibway nation utilized boneset medicine for all bone aches, pains, breaks and fractures by boiling it with hot water and making it into a herbal tea. The Ojibway medicine people waited until the boneset leaves and flowers developed into a syrup-like consistency, then gave the ailing person a tablespoonful of the healing, thick liquid boiled with hot water. Native Americans still utilize boneset, but it is virtually unheard of elsewhere in the world.

CEDAR, FLAT

Cedar trees, like all trees, are at the top of the totem pole and honour us as the grandparents of all creation. Native Americans understand and respect the sacredness of cedar trees and call upon their energy by using them in sweat lodges and for other sacred ceremonies. Cedar is burned to smudge

people who are afflicted with negative energy and other imbalances. It can also be utilized to smudge environments where the energy is dark or static.

The divine nature of cedar assists in healing those who are severely out of balance. As a sacred medicine, it can be made into a cedar tea and taken for headaches and nausea, and it can also be utilized as a blood cleanser.

Although cedar is still revered as a sacred tree, its medicinal values are not acknowledged or utilized as much as they were in the past. However, there are still a few Native American medicine people who call upon the healing cedar medicine.

CEDAR, WHITE

Native Americans gave thanks to the sacred medicine of the white cedar tree. The cedar was taken into sweat lodges and honoured upon the heated rocks. The distinctive white cedar scent was believed to help the two leggeds onto a good spiritual pathway.

The Menominee women pounded the leaves of the white cedar and made a tea from it by adding hot water. They drank this to help them with menstruation problems or any other womb imbalances. There is potent oil in the white cedar leaf that soothes and clears disorders of the womb. The oil is also known to relieve rheumatism.

Its ancient bark has a red hue and the wood feels soft and healing to the touch. Many Native American nations still revere the white cedar tree as a sacred standing person, although its medicine is not utilized as often as it was during the time of the Old Ways.

COLT'S FOOT

Colt's foot was an important medicine, especially for the Ojibway nation. Colt's foot was honoured in the sweat lodge by burning it upon the heated sweat stones.

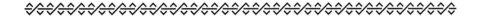

The Ojibway people made it into a medicine tea for chest colds and severe sore throats. Colt's foot was often mixed with other healing plants and herbs to make various healing remedies, dependent upon the physical complaint.

A few Native American medicine people still utilize colt's foot, although it is usually taken with a combination of other herbs and rarely used by itself in present times.

DAISY

All parts of the summer daisy can be utilized to heal. The Native Americans have traditionally used the large daisies by grinding them into a watery consistency. The daisy balm was then applied to bruises and burns and its healing salve helped to cool and heal the damaged skin. It was also used for reducing swelling and as a poultice to draw out infections.

Today, the daisy's healing medicine is not utilized by many medicine people, although a small number of Native American medicine people still call upon its white and yellow powers to help heal painful skin.

DANDELION

The dandelion flower was often used as part of a spring ceremony to celebrate the new life upon Mother Earth. The bright yellow colour symbolized the sun and was believed to increase energy and help blood circulation.

Its yellow leaves also have strong healing powers that help to lower high blood pressure and help relieve disorders of the heart. Many Native American medicine people utilized its medicine by drying the dandelions naturally in the sun. Then the flower petals were ground into a powder and hot water was added to make a healing tea.

This flower was also used to help relieve urinal infections by clearing the kidneys with a strong dandelion tea. The medicine teas had to be

drunk at least three times a day, depending upon the severity of the infection.

Dandelion's healing medicine is still utilized throughout Europe as well as on Turtle Island. It is one of the natural herbal remedies that has been helping the two leggeds for many centuries and continues its medicinal work.

HONEYSUCKLE

Native Americans all over North America enjoyed the sweetness of wild honey. On a spiritual level, it was considered the food of the Energies that they generously shared with the two leggeds.

The honeysuckle was used for a wide variety of purposes. The Native Americans utilized the sweet, watery honey to ease sore throats and, in some cases, mouth ulcers. The honey was gargled for an infected throat and then spat out. Honey was placed directly upon mouth ulcers several times a day until the ulcers were healed.

Honeysuckle's gentle healing is still recognized and continues to be used by many Native American medicine people in present times.

HORSERADISH ROOTS

The strong taste of horseradish was believed to remove dark energies. It was sometimes burnt in ceremonies to eradicate negativity.

The Oglala Sioux used horseradish roots to help relieve painful, cracked hands and warts. The horseradish roots were pounded into a fine powder and mixed with a little water. The healing mixture was applied to the sore hands and warts several times a day until the cracks healed and the warts dropped off.

This healing root is not commonly used today, although some Native Americans still call upon its healing energy.

JUNIPER

Navajo women used to wear juniper berries as protective jewellery, occasionally called 'ghost beads'. They also placed the ghost beads around their babies' wrists.

It was believed by the Navajo, the Pueblo and Tewa that the juniper berries when worn as jewellery or carried inside medicine bags worked as a deterrent against negative energy and spirits. Other Native American nations such as the Ojibway adopted this view and juniper was essential in many sacred ceremonies. Juniper berries were also burnt as a method of smudging before ceremonies and sacred rituals.

Juniper leaves and berries have been gathered as sacred healing medicine since ancient times. Juniper berries were used to clear chest infections, headaches and stomach aches. Juniper leaves and branches were used to heal rheumatism and body pains. The juniper leaves and branches were heated upon a fire and then laid across the afflicted part of the body. Juniper berries were also made into a medicine tea by adding hot water for those who had persistently low energy levels.

The Navajo nation continues to utilize juniper's multi-functional healing powers, although not to the same extent as before. Juniper is currently enjoying a revival of its medicinal purpose in modern society all over Europe.

LAVENDER

Lavender has a potent, seductive perfume, not unlike sweetgrass, and was utilized by Native Americans for ceremonial purposes. Lavender was associated with love energy and many Native Americans called upon it to heal broken relationships. It was renowned for its balancing qualities and its oil was used to restore spiritual, physical and mental harmony. Lavender's healing oil was considered beneficial to all living things.

Medicinally, lavender was used to help heal cut or burnt skin. It was also a remedy to relieve headaches and migraines by massaging its oil into

the temples. The lavender oil was also utilized to help alleviate dry scalp. When used as a poultice, lavender was believed to draw infections from the womb and restore hormonal balance to women.

Lavender is one of the most popular of the healing oils used in present times. Its healing balm is accepted and utilized by people all over the world.

LIME

This green citrus fruit was used by Native Americans to help heal jaundice. One method was to cook a whole lime under hot stones and ashes. After it was cooked it was sliced, and the slices were placed in water. The medicine lime drink had to be taken every morning until the jaundice disappeared.

Lime is used for drinks worldwide today, but few people are aware of its medicinal values. Lime medicine is still used, although less frequently than in the past, by Native Americans.

OSHA (BEAR ROOT)

The osha root is often associated with the Hopi Indians, although many Native Americans utilize this potent herb. There is an ancient legend about a Hopi medicine man who followed a limping bear deep into the woodlands. The injured brown bear stopped beside a green leafy plant and dug the ground underneath the plant. The bear pulled out a solid mass of acrid roots and slowly began to eat them. After the root feast, the bear slept and the medicine man waited. Two days later, the bear had completely recovered. The brown bear had led the medicine man to the hidden healing power of the osha root.

The Hopi and many other nations call osha 'bear root', in honour of the bear. Osha is believed to have bear energy. The Hopi, Ojibway and Oglala people consider the osha root sacred. It is utilized in ceremonies and car-

ried in tobacco tie bags and medicine bags to ward off negative energies and to connect with the bear's energy.

The osha root can be chewed, made into a medicine tea or burnt to help relieve a large variety of physical imbalances. It is good for the heart, blood circulation and the lungs. The osha root is also used to help heal rheumatism, arthritis, migraines, fevers and colds. The method of taking the osha root will depend upon the medicine person's instructions and the energy of those who need it. Osha has a soothing effect and can be chewed by those who have anxiety attacks or feel nervous generally.

This all-purpose medicine is regarded as one of the strongest herbal remedies by the Hopi nation. Osha is virtually unheard of in other parts of the world. Although Native American medicine people still utilize osha's spiritual and healing power, it is not used as extensively as it was in the past.

PEPPERMINT

Peppermint was utilized particularly by the Lakota and Cree nations. Spiritually, it was believed that the pleasing flavour and scent were good for the Energies. Peppermint was sometimes laid out as an offering with tobacco.

The Lakota used peppermint for severe fevers. Many other nations picked wild peppermint as a strong medicine to release toxins from the body. The most potent peppermint was picked and hot water was added to make a herbal tea. Peppermint tea was also used to settle upset stomachs and nausea. Peppermint leaves were chewed to freshen the breath and cleanse the mouth and throat.

Today, peppermint tea is served all over the world. However, this is not the same as peppermint medicine tea, although it is a soothing hot drink with calming benefits.

PINON TREE

Like all spiritual grandparents, the pinon tree is sacred. The Navajo nation revered this tree and utilized almost every part of it for spiritual and medicinal purposes. The pinon nuts were eaten and mixed with cake ingredients. The Navajo women also made butter with the pinon nuts that tasted like peanut butter. The seeds of the pinon were made into jewellery and hung as spiritual protection around the women's necks.

The Navajo utilized the pinon pitch and spread it upon a deceased person's body before burial. This was believed to protect the person's spirit as he or she journeyed into the next world. Navajo warriors also smeared their bodies with pinon pitch before battle. It was believed that the pinon pitch cloaked the warrior with spiritual protection. The pitch was also smeared upon the warriors' bodies in case of fatalities upon the warpath.

Navajo medicine people also utilized the pinon for other physical ailments. One of the most common uses of pinon was for blockages in the body. Pinon pitch was rolled into a berry-sized ball and given to the sick person to swallow with some water. This was used as a diuretic to free toxins and cleanse the system.

Although the Navajo still call upon the power of the pinon tree, its medicine is often left, as the tree knowledge and standing people connection needs to be re-established with the two leggeds.

SAGE

Sacred sage is utilized in almost every Native American ceremony. It is one of the most powerful smudging tools, ridding people and atmospheres of negative energy. The Ojibway, Lakota Sioux and the Cherokee nations utilized the healing sage smoke to purify at birth and passing-on ceremonies. It was also utilized as an offering and as a powerful aid in the healing process.

There are many different varieties of sage, but the medicinal single stem sage has the most potent healing properties. In the past, medicine people

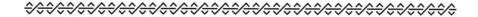

naturally blended their energy with the loose sage by rubbing it in their hands. This is not appreciated in the same way today and sage sticks are used, whereby most of the energy combination is lost through lack of connection with the healer's own energy.

Sage is a potent medicine tea and can be used to help relieve digestive disorders. Sage tea can induce fevers to rid the body of flu and cold symptoms. Sage is also well known for its calming effect when taken as a herbal tea.

Native Americans have consistently used sage in sacred ceremonies and continue to call upon the sage plant. Many people who currently work as healers utilize the sacred sage plant to smudge negative energies.

STRAWBERRY

Native Americans recognize the strawberry as the heart berry. The strawberry has great spiritual significance upon Turtle Island. It is believed to help guide the two leggeds into the Spirit World when their energy is ready to go home. The Iroquois nation celebrated the Strawberry Festival in honour of its spiritual and physical healing powers.

The strawberry has strong healing agents. It can be good medicine for the heart when eaten naturally. The juice of ripe strawberries can help to cleanse the blood and aid the liver. The juice can also be applied to tired eyes to help revitalize them.

Strawberries are enjoyed throughout the world as a delicious fruit, but their medicinal value is not always understood. Native Americans still utilize the heart berry as a healing remedy and for its spiritual powers.

SWEETGRASS

The Lakota and Oglala Sioux braided the smooth, fragrant sweetgrass as they prayed. Sweetgrass' hypnotic scent was believed to dispel negativity and beguile the darkness into light with its sweetness. Other Native American nations also utilized sweetgrass in a variety of sacred ceremonies, including sweat lodges.

Sweetgrass is not usually taken as a medicine, but it is possible to make it into a tea by adding hot water. It can increase stamina and ease muscular pains. It is not readily available in Europe where it is relatively unknown. Native American medicine people continue to utilize sweetgrass almost exclusively for ceremonial purposes in present times.

TOBACCO

Tobacco is synonymous with Native Americans and it has powerful spiritual significance as illustrated. Native American nations have called upon the communicative powers of tobacco since the first sunrise. Ceremony, prayers and ritual were offered by the different nations when planting the sacred tobacco. The Blackfoot nation believed that small spiritual beings tended the growth of the tobacco whilst the Blackfoot planters slept.

The Menominees buried their deceased with a good supply of tobacco for their spiritual journey. The Tewas used tobacco in rain ceremonies as they believed tobacco could commune with the storm and rain energies.

Tobacco is also renowned for its physical healing of the two leggeds and the four leggeds. Tobacco can help to heal and soothe burns by laying the cool, green leaves upon the afflicted skin. The Iroquois nation ground tobacco leaves into a pulp and used it to relieve toothache. The juice extracted from tobacco leaves mixed with water was also used to help expel kidney stones and relieve stomach complaints. Tobacco juice can also help to cleanse infected sores.

Unfortunately, tobacco has been misunderstood and abused by the two leggeds. Like all medicine, if the healing power is not respected and honoured then its energy becomes negative. The Blackfoot, Tewas and Ojibway medicine people still work with tobacco on a spiritual level and also for medicinal purposes. In present times, tobacco is utilized mainly

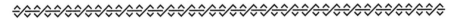

through the sacred channupa ceremonies and as a peace offering among the two leggeds.

WALNUT TREE

The walnut tree, a bountiful standing person, was utilized in many sacred ceremonies. Its richness was believed to fill the hearts of all those present at the ceremonies. The Ojibway nation ceremonially honoured the walnut tree to ensure good harvests.

Medicinally, the walnut tree was applied to help heal headaches and migraines. The medicine person would cut a small hole in the tree and collect the potent juice it released. The walnut juice was rubbed onto the temples and the back of the neck to relieve headaches and migraines.

The walnut medicine is hardly used today, but the Native American people still honour it as a sacred standing person.

The use of sacred herbs and plants can help bring balance to the spirit, mind and body. When a person is ill or feels out of balance, it is often a combination of natural medicines and other healing practices that helps the two legged to regain balance. The following is a ceremony favoured by the Ojibway medicine people to rebalance the two leggeds.

The Ojibway Healing Lodge Ceremony

The Ojibway medicine people also utilize the sacred sweat lodge as a healing lodge. When the sweat lodge is used for this purpose, there are no hot rocks or fire. The Ojibway medicine person and the ailing two legged are the only two people allowed inside the healing lodge at this point. Tobacco is offered to the Creator, the Energies and the sweat lodge itself before the

smudging ceremony commences. The ailing two legged is asked to sit in the centre of the sweat lodge, so that all the Energies and four directions can surround him or her with a healing energy force. The sweat lodge is smudged with sacred sage, then the medicine person and the ailing two legged, cleansing them of all negativity and inner blocks.

Sacred herbs and plants are brought in by the Ojibway medicine person and offered to the four directions inside the lodge. Again, the first direction will be decided by the Energies. The medicine person calls upon the Creator and the Energies to help guide him or her towards the correct herbal remedy for specific internal or external sicknesses or injuries. The Ojibway medicine person asks the two legged to accept healing and be willing to give up the illness. The medicine person sings sacred healing songs and utilizes the power of the herb and plant energies as he or she sings.

Once an energy connection between the medicine person and the herbs has been made, the medicine person can proceed to administer the sacred herbs and plants upon the ailment immediately by laying them directly upon the pain or asking the two legged to chew a sacred herb. It may also be necessary, after the healing lodge ceremony is completed, to make a herbal tea as the Energies and plants have directed.

The sweat lodge is honoured with further tobacco offerings to the four directions. The Ojibway medicine person removes the herbs and plants in a sun-wise direction from the sacred healing lodge. Gratitude is given to the sacred lodge for allowing the two leggeds to utilize its earth womb as a healing lodge. The medicine person places tobacco on the outside of the healing lodge to honour the Creator, the Energies, the four directions and the herbal remedies for their help and guidance.

The Ojibway Healing Lodge Ceremony in a sacred Sweat Lodge is a powerful and ancient healing ritual. However, I reiterate that the most effective medicine is a person's own energy and willingness to let go of illness. Once a two legged connects with the Energy Source, balance of the spirit, mind and body come together naturally.

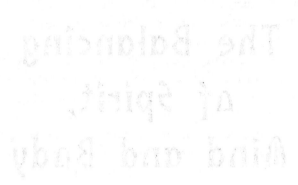

9

The Balancing of Spirit, Mind and Body

To know yourself is to understand balance.
Without balance you cannot stand upright
And your heart will not mend.
WA-NA-NEE-CHE

The days had grown longer and the nights shorter. The Great Grandfather Spirit's energy came earlier in the evening on summer nights. I could see the blue light rising around me as my energy met the Elder. The Great Grandfather Spirit looked to one side and his great grandson appeared. The great grandson was laughing and the Great Grandfather Spirit joined him. The Great Grandfather laid his left hand behind his great grandson's head and gently pushed the energy towards the front. Then he laid his right hand against the young boy's forehead and appeared to pull energy out. The young boy smiled as the Great Grandfather Spirit closed his eyes and sang a sacred song. A sea-blue light surrounded them as the Elder sang. The colour melted into the energy figures and they were gone. I remained standing on the vision plane as my spirit absorbed the healing blue and then I awoke. I felt revitalized and cleansed. I had witnessed a healing during my vision. By seeing and feeling the blue light I had also been healed by the Great Grandfather Spirit.

I understood the powerful healing energy was generated through the hands from the Energy Source. An overwhelming feeling of compassion had filled me as I watched the Great Grandfather Spirit heal the young boy. Compassion unites us at the core and through that doorway, the connection for energy healing is made at the Energy Source. There are many healing cer-emonies and rituals. I would like to share an Energy Balancing ceremony I utilize to help people heal themselves, each other and all living things.

Energy Balancing Ceremony

It is important, as always, to burn sage to cleanse the environment and purify the healer and the person who is being healed. The sacred sage will also protect your hands and energy. Offer tobacco to the Creator, the Energies and the four directions. Then place your right hand behind the person you are working with and your left hand in front. The right hand will push out negative energy and the left hand balances the energy.

Your own energy as the healer must be connected and balanced. You will feel the energy flow and detect any negative currents or energy blocks. If the energy is blocked, use a feather, calling upon the winged energy, to brush away the negativity. Pray as you heal and feel compassion in your heart. You might also want to sing a sacred song or chant. Sound frequencies can be a powerful healing technique when balanced with a person's own specific energy waves. Music and other natural sounds, like the dolphin song and the sea, can be strong acoustic energy healers.

The person who has received the healing can rest for about ten minutes before reciprocating the energy balancing. To return the gift of healing is in itself a balancing of energy. More sage can be burned when the healing balancing is finished to ensure that all negativity is cleansed.

I have recorded a healing meditation CD, *Journey Within*. The healing CD utilizes energy meditation, music, sounds and sacred chants to help balance energy. It also works towards helping people to find their own gift that can lead them to the Energy Source. The following is the *Journey Within* energy balancing meditation.

Journey Within Meditation

The *Journey Within* meditation will take you to the four directions and the four pathways. The energy meditation will help guide you to your own power and to the Energy Source. Sage, together with a smudge bowl and osha, bear root, are needed to help prepare you for your spiritual doorway. The sacred tobacco is also required for communication and to be used as an offering. You may want to keep a journal, so it is a good idea to keep a pen and paper beside you. When the time and energy feel appropriate, write down the knowledge you have received. Describe where your energy and spirit were guided to and also describe the Energies that you met. Relive the feelings that you had and the gifts that were given to you. Keeping a journal will help you remember each journey and often you will need time and retrospection to understand the deeper meaning given by the Energies.

To make an energy connection, you need to hold loose sage in your hands and rub it in a circular motion with both hands until you have created a small ball. As you do this, speak to the sage and tell it what you require from it.

By rubbing it into your hands, you have also placed protection on yourself. Osha is another herb that can be used to enhance your journey. Chew a tiny piece of osha with a pure heart and good thoughts. Offer tobacco to the Creator, the Energies and the four directions.

For smudging, you can use a feather or you can use your hand to wave the sage smoke in your sacred journey area. The smudge bowl is often a large seashell that has the ocean's powerful energy to blend with the land. If a seashell is not available, you can use a bowl, but make sure the bowl is safe and will not break as the sage becomes extremely hot.

You begin by finding a room in which you feel comfortable and where the energy speaks to you. You need to find a quiet room where you will not be disturbed. You may want to use a small pillow to lie your head upon and a light blanket to keep you warm, as your body temperature will drop slightly.

When the sacred sage is lit and the smoke starts to rise, walk around the room in a sun-wise circle to smudge. When you walk in a sun-wise circle it helps to bring balance to the sacred space and yourself. Take a feather or use your hand to fan the sage smoke into all corners of the room. This will clear the area around you and create a place of peace and harmony. When you have finished smudging the room, lay the smudge bowl down on the floor and allow the rest of the sage to burn off naturally. You are ready to begin your spiritual journey within yourself.

As you chew the osha, lie down and make yourself as comfortable and relaxed as possible. Remember, once you have placed the osha in your mouth, it is best to keep it there. It may taste a little bitter, but after a short time, you can swallow it. The osha root will relax you and put your energy in tune with the source of the power. Allow the music to help prepare you for your journey.

You can relax by taking a deep breath and releasing it. Breathe in and out, in, out, in, out. Let the relaxation slowly take over your mind and body.

Free your mind as it drifts gently into oneness with your energy. Release all tensions and thoughts. Allow the energy of your spirit to take away the pains of the mind and body. Become one whole being with yourself, your inner power, energy and beauty. Allow yourself to go deeper into relaxation. Breathe in and out, in and out. You are protected and there is nothing to fear. Let your energy guide you as you travel into your deepest self. Feel safe that your mind and body will always be protected, for they lie within a sacred and protected place. Again, relax as you breathe in and out, in and out, in and out.

Feel the power of the spirit, the power of the energy within yourself. Slowly, let your energy and spirit rise gently from your body. The mind is now willing to let go of the energy and the spirit. Feel the energy rise even higher, let it flow out of your body. The energy is floating above your body. Slowly, let your energy turn around until it is facing your own body. See yourself lying on the floor, lying within the circle, a sacred circle.

Listen to the beat of your own heart. Feel the strength of the heartbeat, listen to the sound, for this sound will reunite you when it is time to come home, when your journey is completed.

Turn your energy until you are facing upwards again. Look up, high above you and you will see a doorway appear. Feel the energy of the door inviting you up and up. Let your energy rise gently until it stops in front of the door. Look at the shape of the doorway and remember it. Feel safe as you go through the doorway. You will find yourself on the other side of the door as you float. You feel a pull from high above. Let your energy lift up, up to the source of the energy pulling you. Follow it to the source of the power.

You stand before the Energy Source. Turn your energy around and look down. In the distance, you can see Mother Earth. You can feel her magnificence. As you look at Earth Mother, feel as she calls to you with her gentle energy. Hear the sounds, the heartbeat of Earth Mother. Let Earth Mother gently pull you back to the earth.

She is calling you to a special place upon the earth, it is your sacred place. Allow your energy to float downward. Let your energy journey back

to the earth as you travel, fill your energy with love and compassion. Let your energy float down until you have come to your own sacred place upon the earth, your mother.

Take time to look around. Take time to relax for a moment. Again, breathe in deeply and release it slowly. Take this time to reconnect yourself with the earth. Look around you, what do you see in your surroundings? What do you feel? Remember what your chosen place looks like. As you stand there, you feel an Energy calling your name in the distance. In a sun-wise motion turn your face in the direction you have been called. You are safe.

Walk towards the sound that is calling you, that is calling your name. You have reached the spot where the voice originated. Look down at your feet to discover there is a pathway. With your eyes, follow the pathway upwards. In the far distance, you can feel the presence of an Energy. You can see movement, you can feel an Energy coming towards you. It gets closer and closer. The Energy takes a form. The form continues its walk towards you until the Energy is standing in front of you. Remember what the Energy looks like. What form has it taken? Be at peace with the Energy. Understand the peace that you have in your own heart and energy. The Energy greets you with kindness and compassion. You smile back because you know that it is here to help you and that you are safe.

The Energy looks at your hand that is by your side. Using energy communication, the Energy tells you to bring your hand up and to reach out. Once you have stretched out your hand, the Energy tells you to open your hand. The Energy takes a gift from the air and places it upon the palm of your hand. Look down and see what the gift is and remember it. Look around you and remember the presence of the Energy.

Take the gift and put it away. Once the gift has been put away, feel a tobacco pouch that hangs around your neck. Open the pouch, take a pinch of tobacco and offer it to the Energy. The Energy nods and accepts the gift. As you breathe in the Energy disappears.

Take a quarter sun-wise turn and face a new direction. Again, look down at your feet and you see that a new pathway forms beneath you. Follow the second pathway with your eyes and look upwards.

In the distance you look for a movement upon the pathway. Something catches your eye and you can feel the presence of a second Energy not too far away. You can feel the Energy moving towards you. The Energy takes a form. This is a new Energy and you feel comfortable with the second Energy and you greet the Energy warmly. The Energy nods and is pleased with your joy and returns the greeting. Bring your hand up in front of you and open it. The Energy looks at your open hand and reaches into the air and pulls a second gift from it. The Energy places the gift upon the palm of your hand. This is a new and different gift.

Look down at the gift and remember what it looks like. Once again, put this gift away. Reach inside your tobacco pouch and take a pinch of tobacco from it as an offering to the Energy. The Energy thanks you and is pleased with your gift. The second Energy turns and as you exhale it disappears.

You have two gifts now, remember them. Remember the Energies that have given the gifts to you. You are ready to take another quarter turn in a sun-wise motion. You turn to the third direction. When you have done this, look again, down at your feet and see a new pathway come into sight. This pathway is shorter than the other two and you can feel a third Energy coming towards you. It is approaching much faster than the first two Energies. The third Energy appears in front of you. See and remember the form it has taken. Greet the third Energy. The new Energy looks pleased and you feel peaceful.

The third Energy smiles and reaches into the air and pulls a new gift for you. The Energy puts the third gift in the palm of your hand. Look at the third gift and remember it as you touch it. Put the third gift away and take a pinch of tobacco and again, offer it to the third Energy. The Energy gives thanks for the tobacco offering and accepts your gift. The third Energy turns and is gone as you inhale.

It is time to take the final quarter turn to the fourth and final direction. Again, in a sun-wise motion, turn to the final direction. Look down at your feet and see the fourth pathway. Before you can look up, you feel a new Energy standing in front of you. As you look up, you recognize the Energy, it has already taken a form, it has already taken a shape. Remember what the fourth Energy looks like. For the fourth time, you bring your hand up and open it. Again, the Energy reaches into the air and gives you a new gift.

Remember the fourth and last gift. Put the gift away. Take tobacco out of your pouch and offer it as a gift to the fourth Energy. The Energy takes your gift and gives you thanks. The fourth Energy smiles and is gone as you breathe out.

You are completely at ease. There is a deep peace within you. You feel free and full of love, understanding and compassion. You have journeyed to the four directions and to the four pathways. It is time to sit upon the earth and to relax. While you sit there, take your gifts out and place them upon the ground in front of you. Look at them carefully, touch each one and remember the order in which they were given and the Energies that gave you each gift. It is easy and natural to remember everything.

Relax as you breathe in and out slowly. Look up at the sky and feel the warmth of your friend, father sun, as he shines upon your face. Look down towards Mother Earth and feel her beneath your feet. Feel her powerful life energy. Feel your own energy that fills you with harmony and spiritual balance.

You hear a voice. You can feel and hear the wind as it blows upon your face. The wind comes as a friend. Out of the wind comes a voice, 'Come, come with me. Follow my voice. I will lead you to the place you need to see. Become one with me.' Allow your energy to become one with the wind. Rise and let your energy flow into the wind.

You are at one with the wind and it will take you to a sacred place. Feel the joys and freedom of the Energy Source. When the wind stops, you find yourself at the edge of a small, round pond. The pond is clear and motionless. Look at the beauty of the pond, feel the peace that surrounds you. Your energy has become as one with the pond. As you stand there, you feel something beckoning your energy. Look down at your feet and there in front of you lies a small pebble. Reach down and pick up the pebble. Take the pebble and throw it into the centre of the pond. Watch the pebble as it enters the water and understand that energy is circular. Once the pebble has entered the water, see the ripples that appear, circles within circles

coming from the centre. Each circle is a pathway of life that needs to be completed. The completed circles bring you closer and closer to the Energy Source.

The pond grows quiet and still again as it returns to its mirror-still state of being. Look into the pond and see the reflections of your friends, the sun and clouds, as they pass slowly over the clear pond. Kneel down in front of the pond and bend forward to look into the heart of the pond. What do you see reflecting back? Look carefully and remember what you see. Once this is done, stand up and remain connected to the feeling of being at one with all living things. You know why you have journeyed to this special place. You have gone to the four directions, the four pathways and you have journeyed to the mirror of life. Enjoy the feelings of oneness and contentment.

You are ready to journey back. Look up and you will feel an Energy calling to you. You can feel your own energy being pulled upwards. Let it start to rise. Let your energy flow back to your place upon Mother Earth. Go back to the place where the journey began. Float upwards to the source of the power until you stand in front of it.

Again, turn and face the earth. In the far distance, you can hear the faint sound of a heartbeat. It is your heart calling to you and the message is that it is time to go home. Your energy starts to flow back to the room.

Your energy is floating in front of the doorway you entered. Go through the doorway. As you come out the other side, you find yourself floating above the room. Look down and see your body.

Listen to the heartbeat coming from your body, calling to you. Let your energy flow down and down. Let your energy be reunited with the mind and the body, let your energy float back into your body.

You are reunited and whole in spirit, mind and body. You have become one and you are balanced within yourself. Lay quietly for a few minutes, then, when you are ready, open your eyes. It is time to write your *Journey Within* journal.

The interpretation of your pathway to the four directions may be given to you on the vision plane. You may come to understand it more clearly through omens or related experience upon Mother Earth at a later time. The

〰〰〰〰〰〰〰〰〰〰〰〰〰〰〰〰〰〰〰〰〰〰〰〰〰〰〰〰〰〰

Energies that you met upon your journey can be described as guides who are willing to help you find the ultimate doorway. The ultimate doorway is the one that guides you to a place of harmonious balance and reveals your gifts to you.

◄

Ancient Native American nations and other indigenous people have spoken of prophecies that foretell the circular nature of all living things. Ancestral prophecies claim that the two leggeds will return to the core and reconnect with the power of the Energy Source that will bring balance and harmony to Mother Earth once again.

〰〰〰〰〰〰〰〰〰〰〰〰〰〰〰〰〰〰〰〰〰〰〰〰〰〰〰〰〰〰

◄

10

Prophecies on a Circular Wing

They Will Return
They will return again.
All over the Earth,
They are returning again.
Ancient teachings of the Earth,
Ancient songs of the Earth.
They are returning again.
My friend, they are returning.
I give them to you,
And through them
You will understand,
You will see.
They are returning again
Upon the Earth.

CRAZY HORSE (1842—1877), OGLALA SIOUX

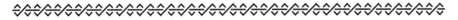

I was travelling in England; I had been guided in visions many times to go to that country across the seas. I was to stay for the night in a little cottage which stood alone at the edge of the moors.

A welcoming open-fire burned and I hung up my wet coat. I sat down beside my friend, the fire. It was raining heavily outside and the rain was blown around by the wind, knocking against the windows. There was a strange energy in that place and I felt the Great Grandfather Spirit hover, before beckoning my spirit towards him.

I do not know if I fell asleep or if I was between waking and sleeping; a powerful place to be, because it releases the conscious mind and the spirit is freed. The Great Grandfather Spirit stood on top of a pale green mountain and I was in front of him. The mountain was bare, except for one tall, lonely pine tree. The tree was unsteady as though its roots had loosened. The pine tree appeared ready to pass over into the spirit world. The Great Grandfather Spirit laid his hand upon the tree. I could see colours vibrating between the Great Grandfather Spirit and the tree. As they exchanged energy, the Great Grandfather Spirit shook his head sadly and gently caressed the diseased tree. The pine tree fell to one side.

The Great Grandfather Spirit spoke, 'I took my great grandson here in a vision when he was a young boy to help prepare him for what the future held. My great grandson's spirit was strong and helped his mind and body to cope with the knowledge of what lay ahead.

'The future is not spread out before us like an endless sea as it was in the time of the Old Ways. No, it is not the same. That was a time when there seemed to be nothing but more time. Now, the time grows short, technology develops more every day and other planets are the new frontiers for modern man and woman. It was prophesied it would be so in many visions.' The Great Grandfather Spirit held the pine tree's fallen trunk and breathed into its bark. The tree became upright once more.

'Look at the top of the tree,' the Great Grandfather Spirit instructed. I looked up and was shocked to see the pine turning black. The Great Grandfather Spirit said, 'It has been prophesied that when we are in the period of advanced technology, and the time is with us already, the trees will turn

black from the top, polluted and poisoned by the two leggeds. It is said that when the grandparent trees have gone, the ancient wisdom goes with them and we are near the final passing ceremony and there will be an end to life as we know it.' The pine tree withered into putrid, black pulp and disappeared into the ground. Mother Earth groaned as she swallowed the remains of the pine tree. A tremor rumbled beneath my feet and I lost my balance.

I came round with a start and gripped the arms of the chair to steady myself. The fire was burning as though no time at all had passed. The wind and rain cast a dark curtain across the night sky. I felt disturbed by what I had seen. The Great Grandfather Spirit had forecast world disaster.

The prophetic wisdom and knowledge Black Elk received through his powerful visions came to me. Black Elk had seen that his people would be starved, diseased and destroyed by those who were prepared to go against the spirit and take life in order to sign their name in ownership of land. Black Elk saw that the sacred hoop would be broken as the people lost heart, hope and life. Black Elk was a wise man who understood his gift.

He had journeyed in the vision world since childhood and he continued to vision journey until he could see beyond the tears and blood. Black Elk saw a time many, many years from his own, seven generations later, when the sacred hoop would be mended. He spoke of the Rainbow Tribe, made up of all nations and colours of the earth with no division, living in harmony with Mother Earth and all living things. Black Elk also believed that a great prophet would come from the East, who would lead the people back to the spiritual pathway and the Old Ways.

Countless other Native American visionaries saw the coming of the strangers with smoking sticks: guns. They saw the men coming from across the sea, encroaching in great numbers to break and harness Mother Earth. They saw their own blood leaking like an underground spring that would eventually flow like a river until many nations were no longer left to tell of their visions and prophecies.

Crazy Horse also had many great visions that bewildered and frightened the Oglala Sioux. Like Black Elk, Crazy Horse saw, through his broken

heart, the end of the free and natural life he had always known. Crazy Horse was only a young man, but he was a renowned and fearless warrior. It was also without fear that Crazy Horse ventured into the vision world and there he saw many things he found hard to believe or understand. It is said that he was shown wheels moving without horses, but they did not look like the hundreds of wagons that brought families who drove stakes through Mother Earth and bullets through the native people. He saw men flying in the sky like birds without feathers or beaks.

Crazy Horse saw terrible weapons, insane greed and power-crazed dictators who caused world wars. He saw all of this and more, but he also saw the return of peace. Crazy Horse saw, years into the future, a time when races from all over the world would come in search of Native American ancient wisdom and knowledge. After that time, every nation upon Mother Earth would join and become brothers and sisters, the Rainbow Tribe, and dance under the Sacred Tree. Wars would end and peace would heal Mother Earth.

A foreknowledge of what lies in wait for us, even hundreds of years into the future, has been with us from the beginning of time. We, the two leggeds, have always had seers and those who could connect with the Energy Source, allowing them to see the past, present and future.

The Hopi nation's prophecies foretell terrible man-made disasters that will decimate Mother Earth. They speak of a Third World War, which will start either in the Islamic Nations, China, India or Africa. The Hopi nations foretell that nuclear weapons and mass destruction will claim most countries, but a small number of people will survive.

The Hopi believe they have been granted permission to continue upon Mother Earth because they have remained on the good path. The Hopi nation prophecy claims that the rest of Turtle Island will be destroyed. The destruction of Turtle Island also symbolizes the loss of womanhood and the murder of a sacred mother figure.

Many Native Americans feel that even the women, who have historically and traditionally retained their connection to the Energy Source, are slowly losing their pathway. It is said that the woman is the teacher of man and children, without her there is no-one to share the spirit of life.

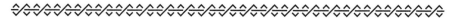

The Hopi nation foresaw the moon landing and warned that the moon should not be disturbed. They foretold that there would be dire consequences if the astronauts interfered with the moon's natural resources. The Hopi nation reiterated that those of the earth did not have permission to remove anything from its original energy source and to do so would create imbalance and universal confusion. However, Apollo 11 returned with lunar basalt, ignoring the advice given by the Hopi people. The Hopi nation believes that the sitting people, the lunar stones, are unhappy because they were taken from their natural source. In accordance with Hopi legend, the sitting people are grieving and their sorrow has cast a shadow upon nature and universal order.

The Hopi people allege that women have the strongest connection to the moon energy. They say that since the moon stones were taken from their rightful home, women have become increasingly disconnected from the Energy Source.

The Cheyenne people have a saying, 'A nation is not lost so long as its women's hearts are high, but if ever the women's hearts should be lost, then the nation dies.' Women have a direct energy link to the moon and, as predicted, the moon is no longer a sacred haven from man's curiosity and frontier-breaking mentality.

An Apache woman once told me her visions were at their most powerful during a full moon. She also said, 'The moon rocks were the children of the moon. If you take away the children, you cannot expect peace in the heart of the mother. It is a sign that earth will have her children taken away too.'

The Hopi people maintain that we are living in the fourth world and it is only when the fourth world has ended that the fifth world can begin. The fifth world will be one of unity and harmony for the few who are left. Many members of the Hopi nation say that they have received knowledge about the future from the 'petroglyph', the prophecy rock in Arizona. The symbols upon the prophecy rock assure the Hopi people that when the earth is shaken and the four directions are torn apart, they will be saved by one man. The Hopi nation believes that this man will come from the East and bring the message of peace, helping them to start a new life based upon love and compassion.

They foretell that the great power will come in the form of a white man with black hair and they call him, 'Pahana', the True White Brother. The Hopi people claim only good will come with this man from the East, but if he comes from the West, he is not the True White Brother and the fifth world will end like the fourth.

The Hopi say the omen signalling the end of the fourth world is when 'Kachina' (Hopi medicine man wearing a sacred mask) removes his mask during a ceremonial dance. It is believed that if this comes to pass, thereafter, there will be a spiritual death and hushed silence everywhere until the True White Brother arrives to reunite the people with the Energy Source. Once the True White Brother, Pahana, is present, all living things will be honoured and everlasting life will be enjoyed as it was in the beginning.

So many prophecies speak of Mother Earth exploding, ignited by man's greed and spiritual desecration, only to be reborn again through the compassion and healing powers of the earth dwellers that remained true to the spiritual pathway. Elders have spoken to me about a place before time, a different star-planet where all the two leggeds once lived in harmony. There was no sickness, sadness or death upon this star. Other planets close by began to war and toxic waste was blown onto the planet that turned bright blue skies to a putrescent sky-swamp.

In life, some people are always destined to escape and breathe new life from the ashes of the old. The two leggeds came to planet earth and asked her to be their Mother and she agreed. Those were the days when the sky and land knew each other as friends and so did the two leggeds. The Energy Source was understood and harmony was natural between Mother Earth and the two leggeds, for to hurt her meant that all life would suffer in the end. As time passed, material wealth and prosperity mapped new territories inside and outside the hearts of the people.

Some two leggeds kept to the Old Ways, but most fed their insatiable need for more by consuming huge tracts of land and placing their heel upon their neighbour as they walked. Fighting broke out and division became more important than unity.

Aggression and lust for power ran wild like a forest fire, killing everything in its way until a world battle began. Then there was another war and in time, yet more wars will rage. We await a clearance.

It is foretold that Grandfather sky will turn upside down and the sea will pass it on the way as it sprays upwards. Mother Earth will sit on her head and weep as her insides fall out.

Many people are aware that we are in a moment of great change, and they try to stick bandages on the gaping wounds we have made in our Mother. How can we heal her as long as the majority of those who make world decisions actively work against us? I believe, we can still repair the terrible damage, if only we unite and work together. If not, Mother Earth will end as we know her and this cycle of life will be over. Some who remained upon the true pathway, may walk through a doorway and find their way back to their original home; to the Energy Source.

All things in life are circular. Our own lives and pathway on this journey circle back upon ourselves. There is no need for fear or sadness as these emotions are a waste of energy; energy that we need to put towards healing ourselves, each other and the head of our family: Mother Earth.

Tobacco Circle Ceremony

Tobacco can be utilized specifically in a Circle Ceremony to help clarify one's pathway. This ceremony also makes it possible to access more information about forthcoming events. As illustrated before, Native Americans perform numerous ceremonies and rituals to facilitate visionary states that help to reveal the future, such as Vision Quests, the sacred Sun Dance, waking and sleeping visions. However, this simple Tobacco Circle Ceremony is easy to perform and can effectively align your own energy levels so that the answer you seek may be answered.

Allow your energy to be drawn to a place that speaks to you upon Mother Earth. Then, cleanse yourself and the area with sacred sage. Offer tobacco to the Creator and Mother Earth. Ask for the Creator to hear your prayers as you ask for clarity and knowledge. Repeat your prayers four times. Then, sit upon the earth and when you are comfortable, let your energy flow naturally and connect with the earth energy. Offer a pinch of tobacco to the four directions, until you are encircled by tobacco. Reserve one pinch of tobacco and hold it in your left hand as you seek tomorrow's knowledge.

Talk to the Creator and ask for permission to call upon the life force Energies and the spirits to come and guide you through time parallels and sequences until your understanding expands and you receive the wisdom you seek. The knowledge can be given in a waking vision or it can come later in visions during sleeping hours.

For those who do not remember their visions, there are omens and signs everywhere, if the two leggeds are willing to see and respond to the messengers. The signposts can come in any form and once a request has been made to the Creator and the Energies, then the answer will be given if you are meant to know it. If it is not time for the answer or future event to be revealed, then it is important to be patient and accepting as you may be shown what you seek at a later stage or you may need to wait until the actual moment arrives. Once the ceremony is completed, you may wish to leave the tobacco circle upon Mother Earth or you may choose to carry it inside a tobacco pouch. If you choose to keep the tobacco, then remove each pinch of tobacco from the earth in a sun-wise direction.

◄

For the most part, it is important to live in the present as that will design our tomorrows. If we respect and honour ourselves, Mother Earth and each other today, we will ensure a tomorrow we can look forward to and a future for all generations to come.

As we live, today, tomorrow and in the future, so too shall we pass onto the next level of energy. The Great Grandfather Spirit showed me the circular pathway of living and returning to the Energy Source. Through the vision plane, I followed the Great Grandfather Spirit's journey as his body grew tired and he prepared for his final earth journey before reuniting his energy with the whole.

◄

11

The Passage from Mother Earth to the Spirit World

What is life?
It is the flash of a firefly in the night.
It is the breath of a buffalo in the winter time.
It is the little shadow which runs across the grass
And loses itself in the Sunset.
CROWFOOT (1890), BLACKFOOT (AS HE PREPARED
FOR HIS JOURNEY TO THE SPIRIT WORLD)

The moment was frozen against the inked night sky. Sweeping blades of black-etched indigo ran like rivers across the earth ceiling. The Great Grandfather Spirit's energy was near, yet it felt faint and distant. I knew this vision was going to take me to a place I had not been before. I had seen a golden eagle flying westwards earlier in the evening. I felt a cold shiver run down my spine as the eagle flew into the fading west light and was gone from my view. Endings and circular completion were the feelings within my own energy.

I lay down, but I felt reluctant to journey to the vision world. A sad energy hung about me that I could not explain. As the night gathered in and spilt blackness across the night sky, I let my energy take me to where I needed to go.

The Great Grandfather Spirit and his great grandson were standing upon a hill. There was a lonely look in the young boy's eyes as they searched the Elder's face. The Elder did not look into his great grandson's deep brown eyes, flecked with gold.

My energy fell away from my spirit as it was claimed by the young boy's living life. Time shot back many years and circled upon itself. Mother Earth was clean with the fresh air it circulated over 150 years ago. We were upon Turtle Island. My energy and life were the blood of the great grandson.

I felt tears of sadness sting the backs of my eyes. Time had moved forward, but my heart moved back as memories collected my energy and carried it to a moment of understanding the circularity of all living things. The great grandson remembered the vivid time of growing and understanding the passage and circular energy of life. The memories and heightened energy etched between this life and the next, lost and yet held in the long, sweet grasses of the summer meadow. The hot smell of the horses they watered was in the air, then the young boy was living within that time once more.

The Great Grandfather spoke of a time drawing close, when he would pass away into the Spirit World. The dying sun had turned to the colour of leaves in the middle of fall as its yellow burden lay wearily in the west. The great grandson looked at his Great Grandfather and although he could see that age had tired him and turned his breathing harsh like cold snorts of wind from the north, the young boy could not imagine his Great Grandfather lying motionless in the earth. In the young boy's innocent heart he believed his Great Grandfather would live in the physical world forever.

Ten moons later the Great Grandfather refused all efforts to prolong his earthly life, but he asked for a medicine man to bring him a selection of powerful herbs. The medicine man came and stood by the Great Grandfather's side. The young boy could hear low, hypnotic chanting. It was his Great Grandfather's voice ebbing and flowing as he sang his passing-away song.

Then the medicine man called to the great grandson and said, 'Your Great Grandfather was a man of honour and strength. He had great courage, he was a warrior, now you must be a warrior. Your Great Grandfather has earned his rite of passage and will be honoured by being buried in the way of his people and his ancestors.'

The young boy walked over to his Great Grandfather who lay exhausted against the buffalo hide, but his eyes were bright and full of hope. The Elder smiled at the great grandson and took his hand, 'I will leave this tired, old body to rest in its Mother, the Earth, in the way of all two leggeds. I must say goodbye to Mother Earth, but understand my young boy that all people are one in passing and in living.

'We are two leggeds and that unites us as one family. I will travel swiftly like a deer to the Spirit World; the Happy Hunting Grounds. My heart is full of joy at the thought of meeting my ancestors and friends who have gone before me. My spirit is free because I will return to the original Energy Source where all things are one and in harmony. My young boy, do not grieve for me, do not let sad, salty tears fall because I am returning to the Old Ways, the days of freedom and youth. I will go back to a time before the sacred hoop was broken and many lost their footing upon the spiritual pathway. I want the days of understanding and unity to be as they were before, when I was a boy of your summers. The youthful heart that beats within me will enjoy the light of the sun and the sight of wild buffaloes without a wall or a fence to break their horizons. It is hard to imagine the bare-footed freedom we knew as children many, many moons ago. I knew every stream and stone like my own family and we spoke silently in the language of energy.

'The grandparent trees told me many things and today, although they are heavy from the polluted air, they still speak to me and many wish to go home to the Spirit World as well. The trees cannot leave as easily as the two leggeds, because their mission and wisdom are so much greater. The standing ones must remain upon Mother Earth for four human lifetimes or much more, sharing their ancient knowledge. The trees are the guardians of the earth and whilst they stand, Mother Earth will survive.

'My time upon this great land is over and I have walked the pathway that was laid out before me. It is the end of one life and the beginning of another. I am returning to the bears, the eagles and the Energy Source. The peace within me cannot be spoken by the tongue, only felt by the heart.' The Great Grandfather squeezed his great grandson's hand with the strength of a much younger man. Their eyes locked together until an energy passed between them like an electric sheet of lightning. The Elder smiled with satisfaction and his hand-grip loosened as he slipped away into the Spirit World.

The young boy held the sleeping hand long after his Great Grandfather had passed into the Spirit World. Thunder broke outside and rain lashed down from the mountainside like great torrents of an unstoppable energy. The young boy looked up at the sky and he could see the spirits of warriors dancing wildly in the rain. A rainbow shone around them, giving strange light in the dying day. Amidst the giant hand claps of thunder came the sound of strong hoofs, outstripping the storm. A shining, black horse galloped towards the warriors.

The young boy saw an azure-blue light in the centre of the warriors' dancing circle and that light grew brighter as they danced and the horse drew closer. Then, the light was taken on the horse's back. The horse flew up into the brightening skies and the rain ceased and the warriors disappeared. The young boy's tears ran down his face as he smiled at grandfather sky and gave thanks for what he had been shown. I also gave thanks and made an offering of tobacco and prayers for what the Great Grandfather Spirit and the young boy had taught me. The Great Grandfather Spirit would remain in my heart like the beating of a drum.

Time danced again and my spirit and energy were as one within my vision. I could see the preparations being made for the Great Grandfather's journey from Mother Earth, but I was no longer part of the young boy's spirit. The energy of the Spirit World quietened and pacified all that were present as the Great Grandfather's new passage began. I woke up slowly and the silence spoke of harmony and the increased power of energy after passing away. I remembered the stories I had been told by the Elders of the Ojibway journey into the Spirit World.

The Ojibway Passing-Away Ceremony

Those who belonged to the Ojibway nation were honoured in a passing-away ceremony.

Tobacco is offered to the four directions and placed around the body of the two legged. The deceased person is placed in a sitting position with the body facing west. The west direction will call as the spirit's energy joins the setting sun. A medicine blanket is wrapped around the two legged to protect and warm the spirit as the journey far from Mother Earth may be a long one. All objects that were sacred to the person are placed around the two legged to help the spirit upon the voyage. The sacred earthly objects were usually a blanket, a channupa, an ancestral bow and arrow and a medicine bag. In accordance with the Ojibway belief, the spirit begins its long walk on a well-beaten path that leads it deep into the good lands westwards. During the first part of the journey, the spirit has to stop and eat a piece of the Oda-e-min, heart berry or strawberry. The heart berry helps to heal all earthly spiritual, emotional, physical and mental pains. The heart berry also strengthens the spirit-energy for the difficult second part of the journey.

Once the spirit has eaten some of this sacred berry it walks on until it reaches a deep, fast-moving stream. The stream challenges the courage of

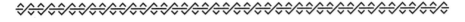

the spirit because over the stream lies the terrible rolling, or sinking, giant rock.

The mammoth rock cannot roll upon a spirit who has walked a good life upon Mother Earth. The good spirits cross safely and once across the stream, the brave spirit can look back and the enormous rock will have assumed the body of a huge, twisting serpent. The serpent shape-shifts back into a rock because its power is depleted by the light of the spirit. If the spirit has walked on the dark side, then the rock topples upon it and that spirit is stilled forever in a blackened vacuum of nothingness.

The good spirit travels for four days and four nights. Each day it goes further and further into the prairies towards the good lands. On the fourth day, the spirit is free as it has arrived in the Spirit World. All the relatives and ancestors since the beginning of mankind are gathered in a welcoming party to greet the spirit. There is great rejoicing, singing, dancing and telling of old stories. The beauty of the place is the same as that of the old days with clear lakes, rivers and streams full of good fish and plentiful fruits. The wild buffalo, deer, bear, eagle and many other four leggeds, flying, swimming and crawling ones share energy with the spirit. All is one and one is all. There is balance in the Spirit World that once existed upon Mother Earth at the beginning of time.

The people who remain upon Mother Earth sing sacred songs. The sacred songs help the spirit on its way. Drums are also played to help the spirit keep rhythm upon its journey. Tobacco is offered to honour the passing spirit and to celebrate the two-legged life spent upon Mother Earth. There is happiness in those left behind because they know the spirit is free and that part of the energy remains with them. In the circular energy of life, we all return as one and there are no finalities.

Eleven days after the spirit has passed, it is possible to make a doorway with a circle of tobacco and sacred prayers. This ensures that the spirit energy is freed and able to go home to the Spirit World. After this doorway is made, it must be closed by covering the circle with more tobacco.

It is possible for the energy to come and go as it pleases, but sometimes, a spirit is unable to make its journey into the Spirit World and is stuck between this life force and the next. The tobacco doorway can be utilized to free the spirit, allowing the energy to find its way to the Source.

◄

Many people do not understand such a rite of passage these days. Death, as they call it, is seen as a terrible and frightening dark angel that steals life in the night. Yet, I believe there is no death, we simply pass from Mother Earth into the Spirit World. It is a new beginning with great enlightenment. There may be sadness for those who are left behind because the physical presence and sound of laughter of that person cannot be understood in the same way.

But, listen to the wind, go where you always went with the one who has passed on, and you will find them if you allow yourself. Try to release the pain and anger that are often caused by grief in this society. The sooner you can do this, the easier it is for the spirit to return and speak to you in visions or during waking hours.

The spirits and energies of those you loved who have passed on try to help you upon your earthly walk. When they lived on the earth plane, their friendship was yours, and that does not change when they pass onto the Spirit World. Yet each one of us has our own pathway to follow and it is not up to the spirits to change and improve that, it is up to us. They will do what they can and what we will allow them.

Once, a brother and a sister came to me and tears flowed down their faces like a stream. I asked them why they wept. They told me that their father had passed on. They said they did not want to continue their lives without him. They described him as their best friend, their foundation and the one person who always understood and was ready to forgive them no matter what happened.

I listened to their sorrowful hearts and I agreed to do a ceremony for them. I explained that their terrible bereavement and anger were holding their father back from the light, keeping him from the Spirit World and peace. They were quiet and sad, then the sister said, 'We do not want to hold him back. We want to allow him to go home into the light.' I could see in their eyes they wanted to let him go, but in their broken hearts they could not cut the physical tie. I performed a 'Passing Spirit Ceremony' within a sacred lodge, and told them that it was possible that within four days their father would come to them in a vision.

A week later, I heard from the brother and sister again. On the fourth night after the ceremony, their father came to them in a vision. He told them he understood their pain and could see what was happening. Their father said that he was ready to go into the light and he asked them to pray for his journey. He also told them that he would always be with them and to follow their own spiritual paths. After their vision, the brother and sister understood it was time to let their father go home. Although they will never stop loving or missing their father on this earth, they accepted that there was life outside the earth plane.

They began to understand that the Creator and each energy make a pact before birth about the length of time we choose to spend upon Mother Earth. The brother said, 'Our greatest source of comfort comes from the fact that our father still lives on, although on a different level and dimension. We understand his energy is part of ours and he is with us in his own way.'

Another man spoke of his severe shock when his girlfriend was fatally injured in a car accident. He said, 'It has been over four years since the accident, but I am still in disbelief, we were going to be married.' As I listened, I realized he was able to cope with his girlfriend's passing. He had faith in the continuance of energy, but he was stuck in the moment of hearing the news of how his girlfriend had passed. His own energy had become trapped in the period of initial shock. In this case, it was the energy spirit of the earthly two legged that needed to be released. His girlfriend's spirit had gone home, but often spirit-energies remain uneasily behind through the grief of their loved ones.

The man and I performed a ceremony together. As part of the ceremony, we returned to the time of the accident and gently released the shock and fear. The man is slowly recovering. He has to learn to release the shock and recover from the emotional and spiritual wound. This will take time as grief and shock can become ingrained as part of a person's identification if the emotions are not recognized and dissipated.

Ceremonies and rituals can help to ease the suffering of the grieving two leggeds and also to guide the spirit energy into the Spirit World. Many people have lost touch with ritual and ceremonies and find it extremely difficult to cope with the physical absence. Some people are even embarrassed about the subject of passing on and try to deny it has happened or will happen again. We have one certainty, we will all return to the Spirit World at some point, we all return to our original energy, but that must not be our focus of interest. We have been put upon Mother Earth for a reason and to fulfil a mission. It is while we are on this earth that we must learn to love one another and give freely with compassionate hearts. We must heal our Earth Mother's wounds and thereafter nurture and protect her. Our journey here is no more or less important than the journeys hereafter.

We are bound as two leggeds in friendship and as brothers and sisters to sustain life on this wondrous earth with dignity and honour. It is the energy that lives on whilst the body disappears back to its roots protected by the trees and the earth. The circular energy of life closes around each one of us like a blanket, as our energy is recalled to the Source and we are all one. For we are all related.

Mitakuye Oyasin.

Closing Prayer

Creator, the evening sun sets on each one of us,
Our days draw to a sleepy close.
All the colours of the night sky beckon
And we follow on its brilliant yellow-red wing.

Creator, all those we have ever loved surround us,
We offer thanks and prayers for each one.
Blue, misty coloured memories of all the days
That we lived and laughed come to us at this hour.

Creator, we offer thanks for all your greatness
And for all the beauty and healing gifts of nature you have given us.
We say only one thing, We are all related.

MITAKUYE OYASIN